THE MEDDLING GODS

THE
MEDDLING
GODS

four essays on classical themes

Hazel E. Barnes

UNIVERSITY OF NEBRASKA PRESS • LINCOLN

Publishers on the Plains

UNP

Copyright © 1974 by the University of Nebraska Press
All rights reserved

Manufactured in the United States of America

Library of Congress Cataloging in Publication Data

Barnes, Hazel Estella.
 The meddling gods.

 Includes bibliographical references.
 CONTENTS: The look of the Gorgon.—Death and cocktails: The Alcestis theme in Euripides and T. S. Eliot. —Homer and the meddling gods.—The case of Sosia versus Sosia.
 1. Mythology, Greek. I. Title.
BL785.B3   292'.2'11   73–92003
ISBN 0–8032–0838–3

To Cora E. Lutz

CONTENTS

Preface

The four essays presented here vary widely in subject matter, but they have two things in common. First, all are concerned with the interpretation of Greek myth and the literary treatments of mythological themes. More specifically, each one involves, in its own way, the interplay of the supernatural and the human. Second, the approach to the problems discussed reflects the particular outlook of one who has devoted many years to the teaching and study of the Classics while simultaneously working with contemporary existentialism. I hope that the result of this somewhat unusual, though not unique, combination of interests may be to provide a new and valid way of revealing still more of the meanings inherent in the rich heritage which Greek religion and literature have provided for all succeeding generations.

"The Case of Sosia versus Sosia," in substantially the same form, was first published by the Classical Journal in October, 1957. I am grateful to the journal's editor for permission to include it here. The other three essays were originally prepared for public lectures but have been considerably revised.

"The Look of the Gorgon" was given on March 6, 1972, as the second lecture in a series established in honor of the late Professor Philip Merlan at Scripps College, Claremont, California.

"Homer and the Meddling Gods" was first presented on January 27, 1971, in Boulder, Colorado. It was one of the Hulley Lectures established in honor of my colleague and close friend, Karl K. Hulley, Professor Emeritus of the Department of Classics at the University of Colorado.

All translations, unless otherwise indicated, are my own.

The Look of the Gorgon

The Myth of Medusa

Medusa herself is not mentioned by Homer, but he knew about Gorgons. In the *Iliad* he tells us that Athena wore a gorgon head on her battle dress and that Agamemnon's shield bore an inlaid replica of the "grim-faced Gorgon." Hector, going into battle glared menacingly at his enemies with eyes that were "like those of the Gorgon." In the *Odyssey* Odysseus says that it was fear of a gorgon encounter which made him flee precipitately from the land of the dead. Enthralled by the awesome sights of Hades, he would have lingered on there indefinitely, searching out various ones of the famous heroes. But suddenly he heard a rustling amidst the thousands of shades, and he feared that Persephone might be sending up some "gorgon head of a dreadful monster." The prudent Odysseus turned tail and fled.

In literature, if not in art and popular belief, it was Hesiod who first provided the gorgon heads with bodies and proper names. There were three of them—Medusa, Sthenno, and Euryale, daughters of Phorcys, and his sister Ceto, offspring of the elemental Sea (Pontus) and Earth (Gaea). Monsters were fairly frequent in those early generations. Full sisters to the Gorgons were the Graiae, the Gray Women. Hesiod tells us of only two of them, adding the paradoxical description that they were fair-cheeked and had gray hair at birth. By the time of Aeschylus, at least, they were three but somewhat under-endowed, possessing together only one eye and one tooth which they passed back and forth among themselves. The Gorgons were human in form except for their wings and their

3

frightful heads. They had snakes for hair, horrible fangs or tusks, and bulging eyes. Medusa alone was mortal. Hesiod tells us that she lay in love with Poseidon in a soft meadow of spring flowers and conceived two children: the winged horse, Pegasus, and Chrysaor, whose name means "He of the golden sword" and who was in turn a begetter of monsters.[1] Possibly it was this love episode which later poets found difficult to reconcile with the horrid snake-encircled gorgon head. At any rate, many centuries later Ovid gives a different story of the young Medusa. He says that she was originally a beautiful girl, famed especially for her lovely hair. Poseidon raped her in the temple of Athena, and the goddess, outraged at the sacrilege, turned the soft locks into live, hissing snakes.[2]

The Medusa whom Perseus encountered was a true Gorgon, an altogether deadly monster. Some writers ignored the Hesiod account and said that her two children sprang from drops of blood shed at the time of her decapitation rather than as the result of amatory dalliance with Poseidon. The snakes and fangs were formidable enough, but her invincible weapon, of course, was the power of her eyes to turn into stone any creature whose eyes met hers. The details of Perseus's exploit, which was retold many times in antiquity, all contribute to the superhuman achievement and the supernatural quality of the adventure. Without divine help and magical equipment, not even the greatest of heroes could have accomplished it. Hermes and Athena accompanied and directed Perseus. Under their escort, he went first to see the Graiae. Grabbing hold of the eye and tooth as they were in process of being passed from one lady to another, he blackmailed the trio into telling him where he might find certain nymphs who possessed the magic objects which he needed for the grim venture. These gracious beings equipped him with winged sandals, the cap of darkness which made its wearer invisible, and a pouch which adjusted itself to the size of whatever it was to contain. The sandals carried him speedily above the sea to the Gorgon's lonely rock. There are two ancient versions of how Perseus was able to avoid Medusa's glance. One says that by luck or by divine plan, he

1. Hesiod Theogony 270–83.
2. Ovid Metamorphoses 4. 790–803.

came upon the Gorgons while they were sleeping. The other says that he located Medusa's position and guided his actions by watching her reflection in a mirror or in a polished shield, a most delicate performance which would seem to require considerable dexterity and some knowledge of the laws of optics.[3] In either case Perseus was protected from the fangs and murderous arms of both Medusa and her sisters by the magic cap. The accommodating pouch enclosed the head so that Perseus could carry it conveniently without accidentally looking at the eyes. Although Medusa's deadly power was apparently known everywhere, there is no record of any specific person who had previously been the victim of her petrifying powers. After the decapitation, she brought disaster far and wide. Blood leaking out of the container fell upon the sands of Libya and engendered poisonous snakes. Atlas, who sought to block the hero's path, was turned into a stony mountain. When Perseus rescued Andromeda from the sea dragon, he either feared or disdained to use his new weapon and killed the monster with his sword. Later in a quarrel initiated by a jealous suitor, Andromeda's uncle, Perseus was so greatly outnumbered that he reluctantly held up the head, turning it against his enemies. They were petrified on the spot, their weapons still held in mid-air. Back at the court of King Polydectes, who had sent him on the heroic mission in the hope of never seeing him again, Perseus once more filled the palace with statuary. Wisely deciding that Medusa's head was too potent a weapon for mortals to possess safely, Perseus gave it to Athena, who henceforth wore it upon her shield. Thus the goddess wears the real Gorgon head as Agamemnon wore the artistic replica.

Perseus is not distinguished by any striking character traits from innumerable other legendary heroes. In fact if we compare him to the relatively complex figures of Jason or Heracles or even Odysseus, he appears almost void of personality. From start to finish it is Medusa who dominates. Or to be strictly accurate, it is not even the whole of Medusa but only her head.

3. Both explanations may have been invented by artists who had to represent the episode visually. The problem is discussed by Edward Phinney, Jr., in "Perseus' Battle with the Gorgons," *Transactions and Proceedings of the American Philological Association*, vol. 102 (1971), pp. 445–63.

Just as the severed head did not decay but continued to exert its power from its position on Athena's shield, so Medusa as a symbol lives on. Like Oedipus, Narcissus, and a very few other characters from Greek myth, Medusa not only has inspired poets, but has been taken up by psychoanalysts who find that she represents certain truths of the human condition. Like any living symbol, she continues to give rise to conflicting interpretations, and there is always something left over. One may look at the Medusa head, if one dares, from many different angles and find new revelations. She is as alive as our thought; she is as permanent and as changing as the human condition itself and our attitude toward it.

The Origin of Medusa

As a Gorgon, Medusa's origin has long been established. Medusa began and ended as a head. Jane Harrison summarized the evidence as early as 1903.[4] Medusa's potent career, Harrison notes, began after she was decapitated. The attached body existed only so that it might serve as a support from which the head might be severed, thus satisfying the rationally minded Greeks. (The story of Alice's experience with the grin of the missing Cheshire cat is decidedly non-Greek.) The specific appearance of this head, Harrison argues, easily suggests its origin. The many examples of Gorgons from archaic Greece all emphasize the staring eyes, the fangs, the prominent stuck-out tongue. The importance of the tooth and eye is reinforced in the bizarre condition of the Graiae, who had to share these objects and who were helpless without them. Snakes were usually present, too, substituting for hair. The Gorgon head, in short, is a malevolent, ugly, spiteful face—a demon face. Harrison sees in it the personification of the apotropaic ritual mask, which has been used almost universally in primitive religions. It belongs with the rites of aversion in which one does not worship and invoke the powers of good but rather seeks to placate or—as in this case—to frighten off the powers of evil. To wear a demon mask is one way of protecting oneself against the unseen demon who threatens. More specifically, it is a prophylactic

4. Jane Harrison, Prolegomena to the Study of Greek Religion (New York: Meridian Books, 1955), pp. 187–97.

measure adopted against a particular malignant force—that
which bewitches by fascination. The Latin root of our verb
fascinate (fascinare) and the equivalent Greek βασκαίνειν both
mean to bewitch, to cast a spell by means of the eye. Harrison
concludes that the Gorgon is the incarnation of the Evil Eye.
The obvious way for the potential victim to insure himself
against the fatal stare is to fight back by making an ugly face in
return; in short, to stare the other down. Although Hector
might glare so balefully as to suggest that he himself possessed
the power of the Gorgon's look, most mortals sought to defend
themselves by representing the Gorgon pictorially—as on
Agamemnon's shield. Harrison points out that these *gorgoneia*
or *baskania*, as they were called, have been found in a wide
variety of locations in ancient Greece—not only on shields, but
also on temples, on ships, even on potters' ovens since it was
feared that the power of an evil eye might cause the pots to
crack. Neither Medusa nor the less differentiated gorgon head
was used exclusively. The Gorgon was but the purest and most
common form of a variety of staring faces used interchangeably
with the simple representation of the eye by itself. Satyr heads,
fierce animal heads, and the face of the Cyclops were especially
frequent. The last of these is of particular interest. The most
famous Cyclops, of course, was Polyphemus, whose most distinctive characteristic was the one great eye, bulging in the
midst of his forehead.

It is not accurate to identify the Gorgon and the Evil Eye.
The latter is more inclusive. Especially in postclassical development, it becomes almost detached from the notion of a
literal eye and is a kind of injurious effluence which may be
exuded, like a contagious disease, without any ill intention on
the part of its bearer. Medusa represents its oldest and purest
form. She is the spiteful stare incarnate. We might say that the
fear of her is the inverse side of a wish fulfillment. "If looks
could kill . . . " we often hear. Medusa's could.

I have spoken of Medusa as a representation of the oldest
form of the Evil Eye. I do not mean, of course, that she was its
original and first appearance in Greece. She is a concrete crys-
tallization of the general idea of the ugly face which menaces.
Out of many gorgoneia, she becomes The Gorgon. Was Medusa

ever anything more and other than a Gorgon? The story of her relation with Poseidon may possibly be taken as an indication that the identification with the ugly Gorgon was a later development, that perhaps Medusa at the start was one of the innumerable earth or mother goddesses who dominated the Mediterranean world before the coming of the patriarchal Greeks. The sexual union of the male sea or water god and the earth deity has many mythological echoes. Demeter herself at one time was pursued by Poseidon and finally overpowered by him. A proposed etymology for the god's name would derive it from *posis das* or "possessor (= husband) of the Earth."[5] Athena's anger over the union of the two might conceivably be taken as an expression of the conflict among local earth goddesses. Medusa's own name is suggestive. It means "queen," a most fitting epithet for an earth mother. Classical scholars have argued that Medusa comes from the period of the matriarchy. Edward Phinney, Jr., in a recent article, states flatly that we should view Medusa, if not the other Gorgons, "as a faded mother-goddess." Of her power to petrify, he says, "The universally known danger to mortals of seeing a deity face to face explains why the Gorgon was believed to destroy all who looked at her."[6] This seems to ignore the connection between Medusa and gorgoneia in general, but I suppose one might say that Phinney has offered a hypothesis as to why a particular mother goddess might be transformed into the already established Gorgon-figure.

Jane Harrison recognized that on occasion the concepts of mother goddess and Gorgon might be combined. She pointed as evidence to an early Rhodian plate of the archaic period. Here a female deity is portrayed in the typical style of the ancient Aegean goddess, the "mistress of animals," standing with an animal balanced in heraldic fashion on each side of her. This vase shows her holding a goose in each hand. But she is also and unmistakably a Gorgon. The ugly masklike face has the typical bulging eyes, tusks, and protruding tongue. The

---

5. For the best recent discussion of the origin of Poseidon as well as of the general topic of the development of the Olympian gods in relation to pre-Greek religion in Greece, cf. W. K. C. Guthrie, *The Greeks and Their Gods* (Boston: Beacon Press, 1950).

6. Phinney, "Perseus' Battle with the Gorgons," pp. 446–47.

Gorgon wings are present. Curiously enough, the snakes which so often accompany both the Gorgon and the earth goddess are missing. Harrison sees this example as transitional.

> She is in fact the ugly bogey-, Erinys-side of the Great Mother; she is a potent goddess, not as in later days a monster to be slain by heroes. The highest divinities of the religion of fear and riddance became the harmful bogeys of the cult of "service." The Olympians in their turn became Christian devils.[7]

Harrison, unlike Phinney, connects the mother goddess and Gorgon as types rather than limiting herself specifically to Medusa. Since Medusa is so emphatically a Gorgon in Hesiod and later, it seems to me much better not to make of her a special case apart from the rest of the gorgoneia.

Thalia Feldman has tried to establish a specific origin for the Gorgon in the matriarchal period while still retaining her destructive quality as essential and original.[8] Referring particularly to Odysseus's fear of encountering a gorgon head in the land of the dead, she argues that *Gorgo* (the Greek word for "gorgon") was one of several underworld demons. Developed in a period when female authority was dominant, the powers to be feared were feminine—in contrast with the male devils in the patriarchal Judaeo-Christian mythology. Feldman derives the word *gorgo* from a Sanskrit root, gar͝g, which she defines as "a gurgling, gutteral sound, sometimes human, sometimes animal, perhaps closest to the grrr of a growling beast." At first thought, it may be disconcerting to find the Gorgon's origin explained in terms of sound rather than sight. But Feldman joins the two together quite convincingly. If the gorgoneion was first a monster or animal head, then the threatening roar would be a natural accompaniment to the frightening appearance. Gorgo "began as a menacing, shaggy feline head, an animaloid outcry, and a devastating look."[9]

Feldman does not speculate as to how "Gorgo" came to be

---

7. Harrison, *Prolegomena*, p. 194.

8. Thalia Feldman, "Gorgo and the Origins of Fear," *Arion* 4, no. 3 (Autumn 1965): 484–93.

9. Harrison (*Prolegomena*, p. 192) cites an earlier article by W. Ridgeway, who argues that the Gorgon on Athena's shield was originally simply the head of the slain goat whose skin provided the garment of the primitive goddess. Athena and Zeus both wore a shield called an aigis from αἴξ ("goatskin").

called "Medusa." Was it merely an honorary title to acknowledge her fearful power? Or was Medusa first an obscure mother goddess who—either in the manner described by Harrison or for the reason preferred by Phinney—gave her name to the Gorgon who became in her own person the quintessence of all gorgoneia? We shall never know the answer to that question with any certainty. In any case it remains primarily an academic one. The Medusa over whom Perseus triumphed was neither earthly queen nor underworld demon. It is not recorded that she greeted the hero with a roar or that she uttered so much as a single gurgle at the moment of her death. Whatever ingredients may have gone into her making, she became finally the silent Look which turns the victim into speechless stone.

The question of origin is a historical problem. To establish, as all of our authorities acknowledge, that Medusa the Gorgon is intertwined with the concept of the Evil Eye is not to explain the mythical meaning of the Medusa head. If we wish to understand what aspects of human experience she symbolizes, we must examine the work of psychologists and philosophers. We will find two radically different interpretations: the psychoanalytic and the existentialist.

The Pursuit of a Symbol

The Psychoanalytic Interpretation

Sigmund Freud (1922) and Sándor Ferenczi (1923), working independently but following the same psychoanalytic approach, came up with almost identical interpretations of the meaning of the Medusa head.

Ferenczi's note "On the Symbolism of the Head of Medusa" is so brief that it may be quoted in its entirety.

> In the analysis of dreams and fancies, I have come repeatedly upon the circumstance that the head of Medusa is the terrible symbol of the female genital region, the details of which are displaced "from below upwards." The many serpents which surround the head ought—in representation by the opposite—to signify the absence of a penis, and the phantom itself is the frightful impression made on the child by the penis-less (cas-

trated) genital. The fearful and alarming staring eyes of the Medusa head have also the secondary meaning of erection.[10]

Freud's discussion is a little fuller and makes a very important addition. "To decapitate = to castrate," he states succinctly and continues, "The terror of Medusa is thus a terror of castration that is linked to the sight of something." The sight of what? Ferenczi spoke of the the "penis-less" female genitals in general. Freud specifies the owner of the dread objects. Terror "occurs when a boy who has hitherto been unwilling to believe the threat of castration, catches sight of the female genitals, probably those of an adult, surrounded by hair, and essentially those of his mother."[11]

The pubic hair, to which Freud refers, might seem to offer a difficulty to the student of symbols. The hair which haloes the face of Medusa consisted of living, writhing snakes. The snake is indisputably a phallic symbol, not feminine. How can we explain the presence of snakes next to the truncated female genitals? All is well. What might have been an obstacle turns out to be one more argument in favor of the theory proposed. Ferenczi, we recall, in explaining the many serpents, invoked the psychoanalytic principle that an object may stand for its opposite. Therefore the presence of the phallic symbol equals its absence. Freud applies "the technical rule according to which a multiplication of penis symbols signifies castration." He adds that the effect of the snakes is ambivalent. For although their presence signifies their absence, the snakes still serve to replace the missing penis; hence they somewhat mitigate the horror.

Ferenczi suggested, without explanation, that Medusa's eyes "have also the secondary meaning of erection." Freud's interpretation of the Gorgon's effect on those who look at her is brilliantly paradoxical. "The sight of Medusa's head makes the

10. Sándor Ferenczi, "On the Symbolism of the Head of Medusa," *Further Contributions to the Theory and Technique of Psychoanalysis*, comp. John Rickman (New York: Boni and Liveright, 1927), p. 360. The note on Medusa is translated by Olive Edmonds. I have written *staring* instead of *starting*, which I feel certain must be a misprint.

11. Sigmund Freud, "Medusa's Head," *Collected Papers*, ed. James Strachey, 5 vols. (New York: Basic Books, 1959), 5: 105–6. Freud comments briefly on Ferenczi's paper in 2: 247.

spectator stiff with terror, turns him to stone. . . . Becoming
stiff means an erection. Thus in the original situation it offers
consolation to the spectator: he is still in possession of a penis,
and the stiffening reassures him of the fact." We realize, if we
follow Freud, that the Medusa symbol both terrifies and con-
soles. It threatens castration but assures the fearful onlooker
that it hasn't happened yet.

Freud does not forget the ultimate destination of the monstrous head.

> This symbol of horror is worn upon her dress by the virgin
> goddess Athena. And rightly so, for thus she becomes a woman
> who is unapproachable and repels all sexual desires—since she
> displays the terrifying gentials of the Mother. Since the Greeks
> were in the main strongly homosexual, it was inevitable that we
> should find among them a representation of woman as a being
> who frightens and repels because she is castrated.

We may note that Freud bases his explanation solely on the
irrational fear in the mind of the observer. There is absolutely
no suggestion that Medusa represents realistically any actual
danger as a source of harm. Nor does Freud mention the Evil
Eye. He indicates his knowledge of the fact that display of the
genitals of either sex was sometimes an apotropaic act. In the
case of the female organs, he pleads that what one fears oneself
may be presumed to be dreadful also for the enemy. For the
male, Freud points out that to display the phallus is the equivalent of a verbal defiance—"I am not afraid of you. I defy you.
I have a penis." Castration alone is what is feared.

I am somewhat surprised that Freud did not include two
other details which would seem to support his interpretation.
First, Athena herself gave aid to Perseus; according to some
versions of the myth, she obligingly held up the polished
shield so that he might use it as a mirror while he cut off
Medusa's head. Does this signify the castrating woman's command to self-mutilation? Then there is the episode with Odysseus among the dead. Just a short time before he fled in fear of
encountering a gorgon head, Odysseus had engaged in a
warmly affectionate conversation with the shade of his mother.
She told him that she had wasted away and died out of longing
for him. Three times he reached out to embrace her; each time

she slipped through his hands like a shadow or a dream. Surely this is an Oedipal dream if there ever was one! Its presence so close to the Gorgon head might well have been taken by Freud as a most natural association.

I do not wish here to indulge in detailed criticism of Freud's partisan view of the significance of sexual anatomy. So much has been written to demonstrate the falsity and inadequacy of the doctrine of penis envy to account for female development that it is difficult to see how anyone not afflicted with Freud's own peculiar myopia could still give credence to it. In the male, pride in the penis and fear of losing it would certainly appear to be natural reactions and emotions capable of being exaggerated to the point of becoming the roots of neurotic fears. But granting this and waiving the question as to whether myths may fairly be taken as springing from the male psyche only, the identification of Medusa's head with the mother's genitals is forced and unnatural, even distorted. In particular, it mistakes the source of danger. It was not the horror of the object looked at which destroyed the victim but the fact that his eyes met those of Medusa looking at him.

But let us turn more objective evidence. How well does the psychoanalytic interpretation fit with what we know of the origin and significance of the Gorgon in archaic Greece? There are certainly some things which might seem to reinforce the conclusions of Freud and Ferenczi though not, I think, sufficient to establish their validity. To begin with, Medusa is indisputably feminine. There are at least suggestions of her connection with the Great Mother: her name, the fact that the Gorgon is sometimes shown in the heraldic position of the "mistress of animals," the presence of the Gorgon on temples sacred to goddesses—for example, the large stone statue on the pediment of Artemis's temple on Corfu. It is true also that the pre-Aryan earth goddess was often represented as holding snakes, though not wearing them as a kind of belt, like some of the archaic Gorgons, or as a coiffure like Medusa. While I personally feel dubious about such laws as those which would make the presence or multiplication of phallic symbols stand for their enforced absence, still it must be admitted that the deity most closely associated with the principle of female sex, the Aegean "snake goddess," is shown with the phallic symbols in her possession. Perhaps the explanation is simple: Possibly the snakes in this instance represent primarily an association with the underworld, that is, with the earth itself of which the goddess is the personification. We know that snakes were definitely associated with the world below, sometimes even thought of as the souls of the dead who lay buried beneath the earth's surface. Or, if we feel that the sexual association cannot be ignored, it is possible that the makers of the cult statues wished to emphasize the sexual nature of the fertility goddess and represented her as the recipient and guardian of the male symbol with which she is inextricably associated. It is also possible, I suppose, to see her as the castrating female who has wrenched his masculinity away from the male. We may recall pertinently that the Great Mother, even in classical times, had her eunuch priests. This would indeed make her a prototype of Woman as seen by many of the patients who come for analysis and—to be honest—of an existing type of woman. She does not seem to me to have much in common with a Medusa who is interpreted as the purely passive representation of the Mother's secret parts which are death to look upon.

Medusa's mother-goddess affiliations may or may not be real. The evidence is tenuous at best. What we know for certain is that in the fully developed myth, her Gorgon aspect was dominant and that the more general gorgoneia which both predated and coexisted with Medusa were not usually sexed. What chiefly bothers me about the psychoanalytic interpretation is that all essential relation between Medusa and the Evil Eye (including all the gorgoneia) is ignored. To my mind the connection with the Evil Eye is essential and only an explanation which gives primary importance to the power of Medusa's eyes is acceptable. Once we recognize that it is the bewitching stare which unites Medusa with all other gorgoneia—male and female, human and animal, and the painted eye by itself—then we can understand why these devices are found in such an odd assortment of places. One might possibly stretch the psychoanalytic interpretation to account for the symbol's presence on the prow of ships, which at least were exclusively piloted by male sailors venturing into always dangerous waters. I really cannot see that the fact that potters were male is sufficient to justify the presence on the kilns of a symbol associated with the horrendous female genitals.

Whether or not it is fair to say that the Greeks "were in the main strongly homosexual," I cannot accept the view that Athena at any time represented for the Greeks a woman "who frightens and repels because she is castrated." Leading her favorites in battle, Athena held up the shield with the gorgon head before their enemies, but there is no record of anyone who was actually destroyed by the sight. Athena's shield seems rather to be in imitation of what mortals carried, an example of anthropomorphism. Just as deities were imagined to have bodies of the same form as those of men and women, so they used weapons familiar to humans. Only whereas Agamemnon's gorgon was an artistic representation, Athena's was the real thing.

Generally Athena did not repel but was the most kindly and approachable of the Olympians. The goddess admittedly was unswervingly chaste. This quality, plus the protective guidance which she bestowed upon her favored heroes, might seem to suggest that she was in some sense their mother, to be trusted and relied upon for help but never so much as thought of sexually. Such may well have been her role in the pre-Greek period, but I very much doubt that this was it for the Greeks of whom Freud is speaking. The usual theory given by classical scholars for Athena's evolution seems to me more natural. Evidently the Mediterranean earth mother combined in her person the total life of women—being at one season the maiden, at another the adult wife and mother, still later the old crone. As she was adopted and modified so as to fit into the quite different religion of the incoming Greeks, these functions were separated and distributed, so to speak, among various goddesses. Hecate almost exclusively took on the character of aged woman and witch; Aphrodite, Hera, and Demeter represented in their different ways the qualities of mistress, wife, and mother. Athena remained forever the virgin maiden. It has always struck me that if the classical Athena is to be taken as satisfying a human desire by way of wish fulfillment, she is not the mother but the eternal daughter. She is "Daddy's girl" who, without ever ceasing to be charmingly feminine, accompanies him in his activites, does not leave him for another man. At the same time she is tabu for him sexually. Or, alternatively, one might see her as fulfilling the role of elder sister. As the woman who shares men's life without ever becoming in any way subservient to them or dependent on them, she might well be a wish fulfillment for one side of women too.

The only story attributing anything similar to a destructive gorgon character to Athena is the tale that when she discovered Teiresias in the act of spying on her while she bathed, the goddess struck him blind. No doubt Freud and Ferenczi would claim that this episode emphasizes once again the threat and terror exerted by the mother's genital on the spectator son. Perhaps, but this does not necessarily involve the threat of castration. Spying upon a deity of either sex was enough to earn punishment. Semele was blasted by Zeus for daring to ask that she might look upon him undisguised. Athena's anger against Teiresias, like Artemis's when similarly glimpsed in the nude by Actaeon, was because of the implied violation.

This brings me to a final point concerning Medusa and the two psychoanalysts. Both Freud and Ferenczi identify petrification and erection. Such an equation is dubious, to say the least. When the penis becomes stiff and hard, it is most alive; it is neither dead nor inert. If there is a sexual implication in the effect of Medusa's gaze and if we are to identify her with the Mother, a more natural explanation would be that the son's awareness of the Mother's looking at him makes him impotent. This view would fit what Freud has described as one of the effects of the unresolved Oedipus complex in a man—his inability to maintain normal sexual relations with women because of the continuing abnormal influence of his mother in his emotional life. More important, in my opinion, this view would allow us to place the emphasis where it has always been in Greek myth—on the notion that danger lies in the eyes by which one is seen, not in the passive object which one sees.

The psychoanalytic interpretation has greatly influenced scholars who have sought to interpret the Perseus myth specifically, or Greek culture generally (what we might call the social psyche), or universal archetypes of human experience. We may consider briefly an important example of each.

Thalia Feldman, as I mentioned earlier, related the Gorgon to other underworld bogeys of the matriarchal period. She attached these figures to infantile fears—frightening noises, uncanny sights like the disembodied heads. With Freud obviously in mind, she went on to explain the development of the elaborate Perseus-Medusa myth as a manifestation of the continuing conflict between male and female. In fuller form, the passage from which I quoted earlier reads:

> [Medusa] began as a menacing, shaggy, feline head, an animaloid outcry, and a devastating look which came more and more to have the power to turn men to stone, to castrate, in effect. To control her power it was necessary in turn to endow her with the body of a woman and to cut off her head, the source of the danger. For that purpose, by the 8th century a myth began to be invented and a hero devised by the name of "Perseus," for his name means literally "The Cutter." [P. 492]

We observe that Feldman, while introducing the idea of the castrating female, ignores the specific equation of Medusa's head and female genitals. I consider this wise on her part. On the other hand, her leap from Gorgo as the paralyzing punishment by authority to Medusa as castrating woman in the ongoing male-female conflict seems less well supported.

Philip Slater in *The Glory of Hera* uses the story of Perseus and Medusa as one of several myths which he believes to derive from the ambivalent relation of son and mother in Greek society,[12] where women were kept in an inferior position but allowed almost exclusive control of the child during his early formative years. Slater adopts the Freud-Ferenczi identification of Medusa's head with the "maternal genitalia" though he links the snakes with the dread female vagina rather than with the penis (p. 20). Like his predecessors, Slater holds that the sight of Medusa is connected with the idea of castration, but he claims that the fear is not of woman as castrated but of the mother as castrating. He concentrates on the metaphorical meaning of *castration* rather than on its literal meaning. In fact

---

12. Philip E. Slater, *The Glory of Hera. Greek Mythology and the Greek Family* (Boston: Beacon Press, 1971).

he goes so far as to speak of Perseus's decapitation of Medusa as the equivalent of the son's castration of the mother. This is a rather bizarre extension of the symbol, in my opinion, though Slater tries to cushion the shock by explaining that he uses the word *castration* in the more general sense of *unsexing*. For him the cutting off of Medusa's head represents the act by which the son effectively separates his mother from her sexual aspect.[13]

Like Freud and Ferenczi, Slater discusses Medusa's effect in terms of the experience of looking, not of being looked at, remarking by way of explanation that what can be looked at can look back. (Such looking is decidedly metaphorical if the Gorgon's head is the same as the mother's sexual organs.) The child, he says, experiences a "sense of uncanniness when confronted with maternal sexuality and fecundity." The feeling is not pure horror but an ambivalent mixture of fear and awe, curiosity and inadequacy. In brief, the child is "fascinated." Slater goes on to suggest that this "hypnotic moment" is not without remote associations with impotence. Rightly, I believe, he feels that petrification is more naturally connected with an impotent penis than with an erect one. He writes, "Certainly the purpose of Athene's aegis was to render potential ravishers impotent rather than to provide reassuring erections." This view is eminently sensible, if the symbol is indeed a sexual one, which I personally am inclined to doubt.

Slater's equating of Medusa's murder with the desexualization of the mother must be understood in the context of his interpretation of the myth as a whole. For him the myth represents a masculine wish fulfillment which he believes to be typical of Greek Culture and, to a large extent, of our own. The child wants to have the mother all to himself. In part this is an erotic desire for possession, but the sexual impulse, not yet fully developed or understood, is overshadowed by fear of the mother's adult sexuality, with which the child cannot cope. The goal is "to restore the mother to the son as a nurturing, nonsexual being who gives all and asks nothing." Thus the cutting off of Medusa's head "castrates" the mother, satisfying half of the wish. Slater argues that the child's ultimate posses-

13. Slater discusses Perseus and Medusa in ibid., chap. 11, "Maternal De-Sexualization: Perseus."

sion of the mother is symbolized by a duplication of roles in the Perseus myth. We are told that after rescuing and marrying Andromeda, Perseus returned home to save his mother Danae from the wicked Polydectes. It is implied that Danae never married but lived on with the newly wedded pair. If we accept this conclusion at face value, Perseus has won his mother for himself, keeping her in the role she originally played for him, and at the same time has moved forward to his own place in the generation series by taking on an exogamous wife for himself—a solution which at least passes for normal. If we look more deeply, Slater claims, we find suspicious similarities between the stories of Danae and Andromeda. Both were cast out by egoistic fathers, both had uncles who wished to marry them. "Far from detaching his libido from the mother, Perseus appears to have married her."

This Oedipal interpretation of the story's denouement takes us rather far from the Gorgon's look. In truth, Slater—like Freud and Ferenczi—seems to forget that what distinguishes Medusa is her eyes and not her overpowering femininity. Perseus, in his view, is a very feeble hero, one with no ideas of his own, one who needs a superabundance of divine help. "He is a phallic nine-year-old's hero par excellence and his conquest of Medusa which, if it is nothing else, is a mythical representation of clitoridectomy, expresses masculine sexual timidity in its most brutal and repellent form." With this interpretation in mind it is not surprising that Slater finds it difficult to understand how the Greeks could take this myth seriously.

> There is, indeed, a deeply comic quality in Perseus' exploits with the Medusa head: one cannot help but smile at the child's fantasy that a view of the maternal genitalia would be as devastating to a group of grown men (including the rapacious Polydectes) as it is to him. The entire legend begs for parody, yet to my knowledge there was scarcely any attempt on the part of the classic dramatists to subject Perseus to the kind of comic treatment accorded Heracles and Dionysus. The Greeks seem generally to have been rather humorless and touchy on the subject of threatening females.

If we were to retort that the Greeks saw nothing funny in the story for the simple reason that not one of them had ever thought of equating Medusa's head with his mother's sexual organs, let alone seeing Athena and Hermes as attendants at a surgical clitoridectomy, Slater would doubtless remind us that the identification was entirely on the unconscious level. But then I fail to see why anyone should have laughed—except unconsciously. Perhaps the humor and the sexual symbolism both are to be derived from the head of the psychologist-interpreter rather than from Medusa's head.

Erich Neumann ignores the narrow equation of Medusa and maternal genitalia but concentrates on the identification of Medusa with the Mother Goddess, which he takes for granted as proved. As a follower of Karl Jung, Neumann is interested primarily in psychological archetypes, symbols which, the Jungians claim, stem from the collective unconscious of humankind, appearing eternally in the dreams and myths and literature of people widely separated in time and space. Neumann calls Medusa "the Infernal Female." She is one of many manifestations of the "Terrible Goddess," who stands for the "negative elementary character of the feminine." She is the "womb of death," the night sun. The dread gaze of the goddess causes petrification and sclerosis. "To be rigid is to be dead."[14]

It would be neither profitable nor possible here to enter into all the intricate network of Jungian symbolism. Neumann indicates that the ramifications of the symbolism in the myth are too complex to study closely. In broad outline, he holds that the Gorgon, a figure in the unconscious, must be confronted if the individual psyche is to be liberated. But this confrontation must be by indirect means and with the aid of allies, specifically of Hermes and Athena, who are the "tutelary deities of wisdom and consciousness."[15] The story of Perseus comes close to being the account of a psychoanalytic cure. The hero seeks out the "ancient denizen of the Unconscious." "He raises its image to consciousness and cures it 'by reflection.' " His

14. Erich Neumann, The Great Mother. An Analysis of the Archetype, trans. Ralph Manheim (Princeton: Princeton University Press, 1963). References are from the 1972 paperback edition. See especially pp. 146 and 166. Neumann believes that the protruding tongue is phallic, like the tooth of the Graiae (pp. 168–69).

15. Erich Neumann, The Origins and History of Consciousness, trans. R. F. C. Hull (New York: Pantheon Books, 1954). Quotations in this paragraph are all from the discussion of Perseus on pp. 213–19.

rewards are Andromeda and Pegasus. (In the myth, of course, Perseus himself never sees Pegasus; the horse was first ridden by Bellerophon.) Neumann underscores the idea that Perseus had to win Medusa before he could rescue Andromeda. He must overcome the destructive aspect of the terrible Mother before he can win the young girl as his wife and companion. The death of the Gorgon releases his creative forces, which are embodied in Pegasus. "What the winged horse symbolizes is the freeing of libido from the Great Mother and its soaring flight, in other words, its spiritualization." Neumann points out that Pegasus later enabled Bellerophon to perform heroic deeds, and he concludes, "Again the symbolism points clearly enough to the victory of the masculine, conscious spirit over the powers of the matriarchate."

I do not deny that Perseus's slaying of Medusa, like any Greek myth in which a masculine hero overcomes a feminine monster, may echo the conflict between the patriarchal Greeks and their matriarchal predecessors. Nor do I deny the existence and the importance of the son's struggle to free himself from parental domination. In fact, I go farther than Neumann in believing that this conflict exists for the daughter as well. I regret that Neumann by making Medusa represent too much, strips away any distinctive meaning which is embodied in the Gorgon specifically. Medusa shares her feminine sex with a multitude of mythical creatures; she was the only one in Greece whose look turned flesh into stone.

The Existentialist Interpretation

Near the end of his discussion of human relations, in *Being and Nothingness*, Jean-Paul Sartre declares that "the profound meaning of the myth of Medusa" is the petrification of Being-for-itself in Being-in-itself by the Other's Look.[16] At first reading we may fairly conclude that the fear of this kind of petrification is less pressing for at least half of the world's population than the dread of castration. If we strip away the technical language and consider Sartre's intended meaning, then I think we may find that in this one sentence interpretation of a myth,

16. Jean-Paul Sartre, *Being and Nothingness*, trans. Hazel E. Barnes (New York: Washington Square Press, 1966), p. 555.

there is a valid appeal to universal human experience and an appropriate recognition of what must have been the psychological factor behind the origin of the Gorgon. Instead of "Being-for-itself," read "a human consciousness"; for "Being-in-itself," read "nonconscious being." Sartre is saying that when another person looks at me, his look may make me feel that I am an object, a thing in the midst of a world of things. If I feel that my free subjectivity has been paralyzed, this is as if I had been turned to stone, made like one of the lifeless statues in King Polydectes' court.

Sartre's interpretation is as closely attached to his fundamental philosophical system, as inevitable for one closely acquainted with his work as Freud's association of Medusa and the idea of castration. In neither case should this fact be taken as rendering the interpretation suspect. Both men selected the image as expressing what seemed to them a self-evident truth about emotional experience. Sartre's view, if valid, has the advantage of applying to all of the human race, not solely to its favored half. It has, of course, its own difficulties.

For Sartre, Medusa is the Look, or at least one manifestation of it. The Look is the revelation of the existence of the Other. The illustration which Sartre uses, the famous "keyhole" passage, has by now become one of the great philosophical myths. Sartre asks us to imagine that we are looking through a keyhole watching intently what is going on inside. At this moment the persons before me are only objects of my consciousness, as completely so as the furniture or as the walls of the room which surround them. Everything refers back to me; the scene is an organized whole with me as center of awareness. I am a sovereign consciousness, pure subjectivity. I do not need to reflect upon myself, for all there is of me is engaged in the activity of spying. I am nothing but this activity. I am the subject to whom all objects appear. This is not a privileged moment of experience. This is my condition, my being, insofar as I am not forced by the Other to reflect upon another dimension of myself. But now as I stand there absorbed in my spying, suddenly there are footsteps in the corridor. I straighten up to encounter the eyes which have already been looking at me as I was looking through the keyhole. There is a dramatic, a cataclysmic reversal. In acute shame and embarrassment I realize that I have been object to another subject. I am not solely a pure subjectivity. I am not only my self-for-me. I have a self-for-others.[17]

Sartre's claim that it is the Look which reveals to me the existence of the Other has inspired a hostile critic to paraphrase his position in the statement: "I am stared at; therefore you exist." If we were to insert the words *I realize* before "you exist," the parody would become a true summation. For Sartre, my realization of the Other's existence as an independent subjectivity beyond my reach occurs simultaneously with my discovery that I, who am always and solely a free subject so long as I live nonreflectively, can be turned into an object for another and viewed from the outside. I may be seen as a hostile object, as disgusting, shameful, attractive, or admirable. The important point is that this judgment comes to me from without. I cannot control it. Nor can I know exactly what it is. The self which I am for-the-other is not the same as the self which I am for-me. It is the only self which the Other knows, and it is a self which I myself can never quite grasp. The Other's Look reveals to me that I am not alone in the world. This in itself might be reassuring. What turns it into a threat is my sudden perception that if I am not alone in the world, then *the* world is no longer *my* world. Worse yet, insofar as I have been in the habit of assigning to other people their place in the world of my mind and emotions, so I find that I am made part of the furnishings of the Other's world. The Look of the Other, which reveals to me my object side, judges me, categorizes me; it identifies me with my external acts and appearances, with my self-for-others. It threatens, by ignoring my free subjectivity, to reduce me to the status of a thing in the world. In short, it reveals my physical and my psychic vulnerability, my fragility.

The Medusa complex represents my extreme fear that by denying my own freely organized world with all of its connections and internal colorations, the Other's look might reduce me permanently to a hard stonelike object. My most obvious recourse against this threat is precisely that of the Greeks. I don a menacing mask. I seek to stare the other down, to neutralize

17. Ibid., pp. 347–48.

the hostile countenance with my own, to reduce him to an object before he can objectify me. In *Being and Nothingness* Sartre's entire discussion of human relations is developed within the context of this subject-object conflict which the Look initiates. We can observe how precisely the Look is commensurate with the Medusa encounter. Neither my looking at an object nor my being looked at by a subject is sufficient by itself. The full experience of the Look requires that I am aware of myself as being looked-at. My eyes must encounter those of the Gorgon who looks at me.

The question will be raised as to whether it is reasonable to assume that so sophisticated and contemporary an analysis could possibly be appropriate for the primitive period in which fear of the Gorgon Stare and, even earlier, the less differentiated concept of the Evil Eye originated. Or to put it more strongly, is not Sartre's interpretation based on an exaggerated sense of isolated and alienated individuality which perhaps fits twentieth-century experience but has nothing in common with the complex of ideas which gave rise to the story of Perseus and Medusa? To this objection I should reply that at least by the time of the Homeric Greeks, the sense of individualism is already very strong. For them the feeling of what one *is* depends primarily on the recognition which is bestowed by others, so much so that scholars have used the term *shame culture* to describe the prevailing pattern of interpersonal reactions. If I feel that I am as others view me, we have the requisite soil for nourishing a belief in the power of the eye of the Other to do me harm. But I do not believe that the gorgoneion is exclusively linked with Homeric society any more than I think the experience described by Sartre is restricted to the twentieth century.

Medusa's stare has both a psychological and a sociological dimension. The Other's Look may be experienced in an intimate situation involving two persons only. It may also be the introjection of the Eye of Society. At least two different ideas are implied by it, and both seem to me an inevitable part of the emotional life of human beings even—perhaps especially—in the most primitive environment. The first is the feeling of being judged or of being liable to judgment. People who pride themselves today on being able to think outside the limits of their

own culture like to describe persons living in a tribal community as unable to conceive of themselves except as part of
the tribe and therefore as lacking full awareness of themselves
as separate individuals. Aside from the question as to how far
we can take this as a valid description, I think it is fair to say
that the sense of close dependency upon the rest of the tribe
must necessarily have been accompanied by fear of a disap-
proving judgment for a task badly performed. The eye of the
leaders of the tribe must surely have been present in the uneasy
consciousness of those who would have to meet it. The possibility of a total condemnation voiced by the tribe as a whole
may well have been equivalent to the threat of disintegration or
of a stony death inflicted by the Tribal Eye.

A passage from Callimachus's "Hymn to Artemis" supports
the view that in Greece the dangerous ugly face was associated
with the idea of judgment. Obviously the testimony of a poet
from the Alexandrian period cannot be taken as proof of what is
said to have happened centuries earlier. But the fact that the
poet is referring to the sort of bogeyman used to scare children
suggests that he is appealing to popular beliefs stemming from
time immemorial. Callimachus has praised the goddess Artemis for daring to seek out the Cyclopes, who appear so frightful to the nymphs. He goes on to say,

> Indeed even the half-grown daughters of the blessed gods never
> look upon them without shuddering. And if ever one of the girls
> disobeys her mother, the mother calls on the Cyclopes—Arges
> and Steropes—for help against her child. And up from the
> depths of the house comes Hermes, blackened with ashes from
> the fire. Then and there the little girl is terrified by the bogey.
> Hiding in her mother's lap, she presses her hands tight over her
> eyes.[18]

Hermes disguised as the Cyclops (cf. the ritual mask) is invoked to punish disobedience—somewhat as the threat of an

18. Callimachus "Hymn to Artemis" 64–71. Literally the passage reads,
"He terrifies the little girl." I have put it into the passive in order to bring out
the flavor of the word mormo on which the verb $\mu o \rho \mu \acute{u} \sigma \sigma \epsilon \tau a \iota$ is built. Mormo
was one of the bogey figures commonly invoked to scare children. Harrison
quotes this passage to document the idea of the Cyclops as a "typical bogey of
the workshop," but she does not bring in the notion of judgment (Prolegomena,
p. 190).

angry Santa Claus has been used in more recent times. Most significantly, the unruly child goddess covers her eyes as a way of avoiding the judgmental stare.

Along with the idea of judgment, the unseen Eye conveys another menace—the possibility that I as a living self-project may be cancelled out and made to play the role of instrument in the projects of others. Someone may argue that this fear could not exist in the communal group before the rise of individualism. I agree that it would not have the same quality as the anxiety of the alienated person in contemporary society. Yet I firmly maintain that another form of it was certainly probable. In any human society sufficiently advanced to have a sense of the mythical (that is, in any group above that of animals guided by instinct alone), individuals must surely envision a future, however limited, in which they will reach a goal toward which they are striving. If the part they play when this projected future is realized is not what they had anticipated, they may find themselves to be objects to external circumstances and persons. The fear of such frustration might easily manifest itself in the belief in some transcendent malignant force bent on blighting expectations, causing well-laid plans to deviate. Even in the rigidly deterministic prehistorical society constructed—or reconstructed, if you prefer—by Claude Lévi-Strauss, myth reflects individual aspirations and deviations which temporarily upset the very order by which the human organism lives. The awareness that I am always potentially the object of another awareness and my fear that this awareness, since it is alien to me, may condemn or transform or injure me and alter my very thoughts of myself—this is the meaning which Sartre assigns to Medusa. To my mind, it has a universal application which is lacking in the psychoanalytic interpretation. In fact if we wanted to treat Medusa as a special case, related to but not identical with the general concept of the gorgoneion and Evil Eye, we could even retain Freud's emphasis on the sexual symbolism. Medusa might be taken as standing for the external eye—parental or otherwise—which induces impotence by arousing an inhibiting self-consciousness or uneasy conscience. I myself prefer not so to restrict the Medusa symbol but to see in it the indication that our freedom is always vulnerable to the

one external limitation which Sartre acknowledges—the freedom of the Other.

One obvious question I have not yet raised. If we accept the
Sartrean explanation of the meaning of Medusa, can we explain
the presence of the snakes? In fact the snakes are no problem.
They offer a difficulty to the psychoanalyst who insists that the
imagery is sexual, for the snake—if it is a sex symbol—must be
phallic. But the snake had many other connotations. In particular it was associated with the dread underworld and the dead.
As such it is easily associated with any symbol designed to
inspire fear. For ourselves there is another natural association
which is particularly apt. This is the folk belief in the power of
the snake to fascinate by the power of its eyes. Whether in
actual fact a snake can captivate or ever has captured a bird by
first fixing it with a paralyzing stare I am not prepared to establish, but the conviction that this is the case is the basis of many
a popular tale. We do not know, of course, whether the ancient
Greeks and the people who preceded them attributed this
power to the snake. It is possibly relevant to point out that the
opposite process, the technique of fascinating or charming
snakes, with music or by the hypnotic manipulation of bright
objects, goes back to very ancient times in India.

In recent years Medusa has come to life most significantly
in the work of the psychiatrist Ronald D. Laing, who has considerably extended Sartre's use of the symbol and has made of
the Medusa complex a major factor in the psychological development of the individual. As with the Oedipus complex of
Freud, the Medusa complex, for Laing, represents a cluster of
emotions and experiences which form part of the life of even
the healthy and "normal" person. If mismanaged it may become the foundation of the schizophrenic personality and
psychosis. While keeping central the idea of being seen by the
Other's Look, Laing gives a new and special significance to the
result of Medusa's gaze; that is, to petrification.

Sartre had pointed out that instead of fighting back against
the Other so as to reassert oneself as subject before the Other
reduced to an object, a person may find it advantageous to
embrace his own object status so as to feel that he has become

only what he is for others. Although retrogressive and restrictive, such an attitude seems to promise greater security. Two patterns of behavior are particularly common reactions. First, an individual may find a feeling of reassurance in identifying himself wholly with the role that he plays, in becoming so entirely what others expect of him that he seems to escape from the burden of having to choose what he will make of himself. Insofar as possible, he submerges what he is for himself in what he believes to be his self-for-others. He leads what Sartre calls a life in the "spirit of seriousness," an unauthentic existence.

A second possibility is that a person may form an image of what he believes or wishes to be his true self and then seek to conform to it in every way. In this case he "petrifies" certain aspects of himself as the "real self." This is what he is. He neither can nor will be anything else. For the sake of clinging to the known and familiar, he refuses to allow for any possibility of change, growth, or spontaneity. For Sartre, both of these conducts are devices in bad faith; he has not associated them with the name of Medusa. In each instance, more obviously in the second pattern, one could, I believe, say that the individual has made himself into a Medusa and destroyed himself by his own Look. Medusa proves to be first cousin to Narcissus.

Presented most fully in *The Divided Self*, Laing's description of the Medusa complex includes and extends both of these patterns.[19] Laing finds that some persons may suffer from what he calls "ontological insecurity"; that is, one has no firm feeling or understanding of oneself as a unique, separate being whose existence is sure. In his human relations his very being is threatened, as though he might be absorbed or devoured by the Other. He is terrified lest others steal his thoughts or, on the other hand, might implant their thoughts inside him like a fifth column to usurp his personality and take over his life. Laing classifies these fears in three categories. The ontologically insecure person may fear engulfment, in which he is lost in others; implosion, whereby his empty self might be crushed by the impingement of reality; and petrification. It is the third of these, of course, which Laing develops in terms of the Medusa complex.

19. R. D. Laing, *The Divided Self: An Existential Study in Sanity and Madness* (London: Tavistock Publications, 1959).

Laing's discussion is introduced in the context of the study of schizoid behavior and potential schizophrenics. He finds that the germ of psychosis lies in the experience or the fear of being treated as an object, as a depersonalized "it" by one or more other persons. One may feel a sense of panic in all human relations as if his vulnerable self would be petrified in any personal encounter. One recourse, particularly easy for the ontologically insecure, is to assume a mask, to refuse to put "the real self" into any overt conduct, to pretend that the "I" is not the self who acts and is seen by others. So far we have the classic response to the Gorgon's threat: by wearing a face that is not his own, the anxious individual practices a protective deception. But what of the "real self"? This, Laing says, is hidden deep within, out of reach of any menacing Look. But since it is cut off from all contact with the external world, it becomes increasingly more empty and abstract, enjoying freedom only in fantasy which, because it is not nourished by anything real, can never be truly satisfying. The "real self" is denied all possibility of growth, paralyzed and petrified by overprotection. What the external Look of Medusa could not touch is turned to stone by the inner eye of the victim.

Laing does not hold that this neurotic conduct is irrational and incomprehensible. On the contrary, he argues that if we examine the families of so-called schizophrenics, we frequently find that the responses of the schizoid are entirely appropriate and understandable in their context. Even the ultimate psychosis may be seen as the result of a perfectly logical formation. Laing, more than all others of the commentators on Medusa, argues that the Gorgon's stare is in very truth a source of the greatest danger. Society, by fixing its accusing Look on the child Genet, simultaneously robbed him of his right to live as a free being and constituted him a thief. Classifications by race, sex, or class threaten to imprison us in a role which the Other has defined. So does the intricate net of expectations and demands with which parents seek to bind their children to them. In my most intimate relations I cannot escape the knowledge that the Other sees me as something (some thing); this awareness colors my sense of what in truth I am. My idea of what I am may lead me to become it. This view of interpersonal relations is the underlying thesis of Laing's book *Knots*, that strange combination of poetry and almost mathematical analysis of what humans do to one another and to themselves.

> Narcissus fell in love with his image, taking it to
> be another.
>
> Jack falls in love with Jill's image of Jack, taking
> it to be himself.
> She must not die, because then he would lose himself.
> He is jealous in case any one else's image is reflected in her
> mirror.
>
> Jill is a distorting mirror to herself.
> Jill has to distort herself to appear undistorted
> to herself.
>
> To undistort herself, she finds Jack to distort her
> distorted image in his distorting mirror
> She hopes that his distortion of her distortion may
> undistort her image without her having to distort herself.[20]

In this psychological play of mirrors, Laing presents at least three models for using the Look in the game of Self and Other. Narcissus convinces himself that what is in reality the freely created projection of himself comes to him with the support of external guarantee. Through too much devotion to the beloved object, he loses all free mobility and ultimately his life. Jack identifies himself with a particular self-for-the-other which is reflected to him by Jill. His pride in himself is nourished by the image which she sustains but paid for by his neurotic dependency and jealous anxiety. Jill finds herself incapable of being spontaneously what she might be without the superimposition of a determining image. Finding no inner support for her own authentic being, and afraid to confront the self which she might find if she looked without a distorted lens, Jill relies on Jack to take over the responsibility for what she is. Thus Narcissus kills himself with his own Look, Jack looks at Jill's image of him and calls it himself, and Jill nervously hopes that Jack's Look will create an image which might turn out to be real.

The Afterlife of Medusa

If we consider some of Medusa's appearances at various points

20. R. D. Laing, *Knots* (New York: Pantheon Books, 1970), p. 31. Copyright © 1970 by R. D. Laing. Reprinted by permission of Pantheon Books, a Division of Random House, Inc.

in literary and artistic history, I think we shall find that the sense of external judge and observer is constant and uppermost. In the Mediterranean world, the still living concept of the Evil Eye has accumulated a complex of fears and prophylactic devices almost infinitely large in scope and extremely vague. Persistent and central is the feeling that a hostile force emanates from the presence of a person or from a personal force, visible or invisible. The most common of all antidotes is the blue bead, placed by tender guardians on the necks of babies or donkeys or around whatever is especially valued. Nobody seems to know exactly what makes the bead effective. It has been said that the "eyes" of the beads may serve to divert the Evil Eye from those whom it would otherwise injure.[21] But why is the bead blue? The round blue object might be taken as resembling the pupil of the hostile stranger's eye. One theory would connect it with the fact that it was the blue-eyed Aryan invaders who became the ruling class in Greece and who would consequently be most feared by the native population. This view, though not impossible, seems to me rather too precisely dated to explain so general and so long-lasting a practice. An alternative, which I offer as speculation only, is that the bead is blue because the sky is blue—especially along the Mediterranean. The sense of an unseen presence watching and judging one has resulted in two quite different phenomena. One is the introjection of Society's Eye—what Freud calls the superego. The other is the anthropomorphizing of the Heavens. In classical Greece we find repeated references to the "all-seeing Sun," not a hostile being but the impartial deity from whom no secrets are hid. In popular Christianity God himself is located at a vantage point "up there." I am convinced that there is a definite connection between the Evil Eye and the Eye of God which appears so often in the dome of the Byzantine church. Sometimes the face of God is depicted, occasionally his entire figure; often we find the eye by itself, indistinguishable in appearance from the eye found on ancient Greek vases. Obviously the Eye of God has lost all connotation of wicked malevolence, but this does not mean that it is wholly benign and protective. It is still the Eye which judges the sinner and warns the faithful that they must remain true. Even the protec-

21. Phinney, "Perseus' Battle with the Gorgons," p. 445.

tiveness may imply hostility toward the enemies of those who worship, just as the figure of the Gorgon on Artemis's temple must have done. I confess that I cannot, by the utmost stretch of the imagination, relate the Byzantine Eye of God to the Medusa head as it has been interpreted psychoanalytically. But as I have stated earlier, one of my objections to that view is the fact that it so radically separates Medusa from the rest of the gorgoneia.

Returning to Medusa specifically, I find a most significant use of the symbol in Dante's *Inferno*. In canto 9 Virgil and Dante encounter her as they stand outside the walls of the city of Dis. The devils have refused to allow them to enter the gates of Lower Hell. While Virgil and Dante await the aid of the Heavenly Messenger, the devils seek to prevent their advance by holding up Medusa's head. This is the only occasion during the entire journey that Virgil is seriously frightened. He tells Dante to close his eyes and to hold his fingers tightly over them; Virgil presses his hands over Dante's. We cannot adequately explain this behavior as simply a device to create suspense. When Dante employs a figure from classical myth, he always uses it symbolically in such a way that its earlier meaning and the Christian allegory work hand in hand. In the case of Minos, for example, although Dante has turned him into a monstrous dragon, he still functions as an underworld judge just as he did for the Greeks. But in Dante's Christian Hell, Minos's role is reduced to that of an automaton. He carries out the judgment of God mechanically by wrapping his tail around his body in as many coils as required to indicate the number of the circle to which each sinner is destined. I think that similarly Medusa is an instrument of God's purpose. Here the image is subtly adapted to Dante's particular situation (I mean Dante, the character, of course, not the author). Dante, while still living, has been granted by divine command the privilege of exploring Hell. The author's point, if I understand him correctly, is that Medusa represents the divine judgment which fixes the sinner for eternity, with no further possibility of redemption, in the place for which his life has prepared him. That is why Virgil must at all cost prevent Dante from meeting Medusa's eyes. The allegorical journey will allow Dante to look

into himself and discover within him the possibilities for all
sin, which gradually he will uproot. By ascending through
Purgatory and Paradise, he—like the souls of those whom he
encounters—will be purified of sin and inspired to foster those
qualities which link mortal and divine. After this careful prep-
aration, he will be able to look upon the face of God himself.
But Dante must not confront divine judgment at this early stage
of the journey. If he faces the eye of final judgment before he
has explored his soul and repented, he must stay in Hell forever
in whatever circle best fits his chosen way of error.[22]

A later example, from an equally famous source, underscores the idea that Medusa's head represents the Eye which
appraises my conduct and condemns it. This is found in part 1
of Goethe's *Faust*. Mephistopheles and Faust have been par-
ticipating in a glorious revel with the witches and other evil
spirits on Walpurgis Night. Suddenly Faust is bored and wants
to leave. Questioned by Mephistopheles about the reason for
this unexpected shift in mood, Faust explains:

Faust. Mephistopheles, do you see over there a pale, beautiful girl
standing alone and apart? She advances, but slowly, and appears to
be walking with her feet in chains. I must confess that she seems to
me to look very much like Gretchen.
Mephistopheles. Let her stand there! This won't do you any good.
She is a magic image, lifeless, a phantom. It is bad to encounter her.
A man's blood congeals at her staring gaze, and he can well be
turned to stone. You have heard of Medusa, haven't you?
Faust. Indeed they are the eyes of a dead person which no loving
hand has closed. That is the breast which Gretchen offered to me.
That is the sweet body which I enjoyed.
Mephistopheles. It's sorcery, you gullible fool! You see, everybody
mistakes her for his own love.[23]

At this moment Gretchen is in prison for the murder of her
illegitimate child. Although Faust does not know the full ex-

22. Dorothy L. Sayers in commenting on Medusa says that "she is the
image of despair which so hardens the heart that it becomes powerless to
repent." Despite my almost unbounded admiration for Sayers's work on Dante,
I find this interpretation totally unsatisfactory. It has no reference whatsoever
to Medusa's role for the Greeks nor any support in its specific context in
Dante's epic. Cf. Sayers's translation, *The Divine Comedy*, vol. 1, *Hell*
(Baltimore: Penquin Books, 1949), p. 127.
23. Johann Wolfgang von Goethe, *Faust*, pt. 1, ll. 4183–4200.

tent of her misery, he is well aware that he has brought her unhappiness. Medusa, who takes on the form of any man's love, represents Faust's involuntary, conscience-stricken remembrance of Gretchen, of what he has done to her, and of what their love affair and his subsequent actions have been if looked at from her point of view. He feels guilty for having forgotten her; the revelry in which he has recently indulged takes on a new aspect. Medusa's stare, as Goethe treats it, stands midway between the Other's judgment and the judgment of conscience in which I myself assume the Eye of the Other.

This same combination of projection and introjection appears in a passage from Tillich's *The Courage to Be*. Neither Medusa nor the Evil Eye is mentioned in so many words. The book was written nearly ten years later than Sartre's *Being and Nothingness* and may possibly reflect some Sartrean influence. Nevertheless Tillich's remarks seem to me to confirm some of the associations which I have been making. In the context he is criticizing violently (for him) the traditional view of God as the external judge, the subject before whom I am a helpless object.

> God as a subject makes me into an object which is nothing more than an object. He deprives me of my subjectivity because he is all-powerful and all-knowing. I revolt and try to make him into an object, but the revolt fails and becomes desperate. God appears as the invincible tyrant. . . . He becomes the model of everything against which Existentialism revolted. This is the God Nietzsche said had to be killed because nobody can tolerate being made into a mere object of absolute knowledge and absolute control.[24]

We note that the attempted remedy against the Look of the Absolute Subject is once again to don the apotropaic Look —that is, to put on the ritual mask.

Medusa has been used as a symbol in another context which overtly, at least, is neither psychoanalytic nor Sartrean. Two writers have chosen to use her to symbolize art or the enterprise of the artist.

24. Paul Tillich, *The Courage to Be* (New Haven: Yale University Press, 1959), p. 185.

In a book of short stories, *Youth and the Bright Medusa*, Willa Cather has picked up the implications of the tale of the young Medusa, the girl with the beautiful hair who preceded the snake-entwined Gorgon. At the same time Cather has retained the idea of the petrifying Look. The ambivalence of the relation between art and life comes out most strongly. In some of the stories the central character's human relations have been sacrificed to the artist's struggle for recognition. The inner life and personality have been partially dehumanized and hardened—turned to stone. "Coming, Aphrodite" ends with the description of the recognized prima donna.

> Leaning back in the cushions, Eden Bower closed her eyes, and her face, as the street lamps flashed their ugly orange light upon it, became hard and settled, like a plaster cast; so a sail, that has been filled by a strong breeze, behaves when the wind suddenly dies. Tomorrow night the wind would blow again, and this mask would be the golden face of Aphrodite. But a "big" career takes its toll, even with the best of luck.[25]

In other stories—for example, "Scandal," "The Diamond Mine," "The Sculptor's Funeral"—the artist is vitally alive and creative. It is the small-minded Philistines who seek to exploit or to degrade him—to use him as an instrument to further their own projects or to transform him by their Look into an object of contempt. In "Paul's Case" the boy's preference for the illusionary world of opera and theater leads him to theft, a brief moment of glorious role playing, and suicide. Art—seen falsely to be sure—brings death. Most ambivalent of all the stories is "A Wagner Matinee," in which the heroine, an elderly woman isolated for many years in a prairie settlement, returns to Boston for a visit. When her nephew takes her to a concert, she is simultaneously exalted and grief-stricken, overcome by the pain of realizing what she has missed. In this story art seems to be what gives glory to life, but Aunt Georgiana's brief awakening to the beauty of the bright Medusa promises henceforth to poison her bleak existence for so long as she will live.

25. I am grateful to Bernice Slote for drawing my attention to this collection of short stories. Willa Cather, *Youth and the Bright Medusa* (New York: Alfred A. Knopf, 1920). It is interesting to note that Hedger, before the two became lovers, had spied on Eden through a knothole in his closet. Unlike the watcher in Sartre's example, he was not caught in the act.

The association of both beauty and death with the Medusa head is not entirely foreign to the Greeks, even aside from the account of the young girl who entranced Poseidon. Beauty plays no part in the Perseus myth as it was represented in the archaic period; there the Gorgon's monstrous ugliness is unrelieved. In the fifth century B.C. artists began to emphasize the pathos of Medusa, who was portrayed as peacefully sleeping when Perseus approached her. By the Hellenistic period she is once again a beautiful woman. Fangs, stuck-out tongue, and bulging eyes are gone. If the snakes remain, as they sometimes do, they are no longer grotesque; subdued in a carefully arranged coiffure encircling Medusa's face, they strengthen the effect of a truly deadly beauty. Hers is a face which it is death to look upon but which lures us to it, a representation of *fascination* with the ambivalent meaning which the English word holds for us today.

Considered from this point of view, the "bright Medusa" seems to me to express perfectly not only Willa Cather's own mixed feelings concerning the artist's dedication but an ambivalence which stems from the very nature of art. It is possible to see in the Gorgon's Look the apotheosis of artistic achievement. The transformation of flesh into stone might be viewed, not as a passage from life to death but as the imposition of beauty and form upon the chaotic flux of experience. Yet to prefer literature to life, illusion to reality, to view one's life as if it were something made and finished like the artistic object—this is to kill what is human and alive in us.

Historically, the link between Medusa and art is reinforced by, if it does not derive from, the fact that one of her sons by Poseidon was Pegasus. We can only speculate as to how and why the Gorgon's offspring should become the symbol of poetry. My guess would be that the origin of the winged horse was entirely prosaic and that the rich metaphorical meanings associated with him were a secondary development which took place only gradually. His name is derived from πηγή, a "spring." Though Hesiod tells us that he was called "Pegasus" because he was born near the springs of Ocean,[26] a more scholarly explanation points to the association of Pegasus's father with springs. Poseidon, according to some authorities, was god

26. Hesiod *Theogony* 281–83.

of the waters beneath the earth long before he took over the sea. We may note also that the horse was closely associated with Poseidon and that on at least one occasion the god appeared in the guise of a horse. An archaic vase shows Medusa herself in the form of a female centaur.[27] Possibly the artist was influenced by the tale that she was Pegasus's mother. Or he may have confused her story with that of Demeter, who once assumed the shape of a mare to escape the pursuing Poseidon, only to be captured by him in the form of a stallion. In any case the Gorgons had wings. A winged horse is an altogether appropriate form for the hybrid offspring of Medusa and Poseidon. If this unpoetic explanation is offensive to those for whom Pegasus is so perfect an expression of the poet's imagination that he might almost be called a "natural symbol"—like the tree of life—let me add quickly that the later development seems to me both natural and inevitable. The idea of the spring as a source of inspiration, and the association between poetic fantasy and the horse which bore the hero on heroic exploits and which could fly up toward Heaven itself—these must speedily and most naturally have led to Pegasus's becoming the favored pet of the Muses. But I believe this was his destination or destiny, so to speak, rather than his point of origin.

I have allowed myself to digress apropos of Pegasus, partly because he furnishes the implied connection between art and Ovid's lovely haired girl, and partly because he is essential to the symbolism invoked by another writer who has related Medusa and art. Kimon Friar, in an essay "The Stone Eyes of Medusa,"[28] does not try to justify his interpretation as being in actual fact either the explanation of the origin of the Perseus-Medusa story or its objective meaning. He is content to dis-

27. If indeed the identification is correct, which is debatable. Jocylyn M. Woodward provides a reproduction of the vase and discusses it in *Perseus: A Study in Greek Art and Legend* (Cambridge: At the University Press, 1937), pp. 31–32. More recently John Boardman has commented on four gems from the sixth century B.C., all of them depicting a monster with Gorgon head and horse's body. In each instance the creature is grappling with another animal, but there is no sign of Perseus. It seems to me most likely that this is not Medusa but merely one of many hybrid demon like figures which the Greeks developed, probably under the influence of the art of Egypt and the Orient. Boardman, *Archaic Greek Gems: Schools and Artists in the Sixth Century B.C.* (London: Thames and Hudson, 1968), pp. 27–28.

28. Kimon Friar, "The Stone Eyes of Medusa," *Greek Heritage* 6 (1965): 26–39.

cover in the myth what he personally believes to be an "adequate symbol to evoke what I consider to be the complexity of artistic purpose." For Friar, Perseus is The Poet. The challenge given to him by Polydectes "is the dare which the world at large is always casting before young men of imagination as they go unready to face the odds of the physical world, whether in the form of primeval monsters or the more monstrous machines of modern warfare and of robot institutions." Friar interprets other details of the story in a manner closer to personal allegory, as he himself admits, than to "the evocation of symbolism." Hermes, for example, is "the medium between poets and the infinities." Athena "represents that synthesis of creative wisdom which must come before any action." The Graiae, the only ones who can direct Perseus to Medusa's dwelling place, stand for "the historical past, the schools and the universities, the academies of learning where knowledge is frozen fast in unyielding rigidity." From them The Poet must learn direction and perspective, but eventually he must make of their eye his own "instrument of perception," must seize their one tooth, which is "their sole masticating tool of history, but his divinatory organ." This and much related matter is of importance to persons interested in Kimon Friar rather than in the pursuit of the Gorgon. What Friar says of Medusa herself and of her decapitation is more relevant to our purpose. Referring specifically to the later beautiful Medusa, Friar sees in her the symbol of "perfection in its absolute form, pattern devoid of subject." "She is pure form, the object of art as it is dreamed, not as it is materialized in the actual world. . . . She is art for art's sake, the pursuit of perfection, and in her finality she is Death." Friar calls her also the mask of the poet's antithesis. He says that The Poet who meets her hypnotic glance "gazes into that portion of Evil before which every artist must shudder in temptation. He stares not into the moral or the immoral eyes of humanity, but into the blank and amoral gaze of indifferent nature." How Medusa can be quite all of these things at once is not altogether clear to me, and I suspect that Friar prizes his symbol more for its rich suggestion than for its clarity. At any rate she stands for the antithesis of The Poet's individual vision. The sight of her represents something between Nietzsche's

Dionysian vision of a universe which is eternal but meaningless for the human individual, and the mystic's vision of a
higher reality in which self and the manifold world are lost.
Hence if The Poet confronts her directly, he may either "drown
like Narcissus ... in the madness of introversion" or be
brought to renounce poetry for sainthood. Yet because Medusa
stands for some kind of suprahuman abstract truth, The Poet
must encounter her, though indirectly, by looking at her image
in Athena's shield. When he has thus glimpsed the forbidden
image without allowing himself to be captivated by it,
Pegasus—the poem or the work of art—is born.

At this point we may ask whether Kimon Friar's highly
personal interpretation and Willa Cather's more objective but
still individual use of the Medusa head have any relevance to
the Medusa complex as treated by psychologists, either
psychoanalytic or existentialist. Or do they simply illustrate
the fact that a myth cannot be interpreted so as to distill from it
any "true" meaning but rather may serve to support any meaning one chooses to impose upon it—like a material object
which the poet transforms into his private image?

I do not believe that either writer has found the symbol
significant in the sexual terms suggested by the psychoanalysts. Willa Cather is certainly aware of the link between
the erotic impulse and artistic creativity but in a manner closer
to Plato than to Freud. Kimon Friar, who is acquainted with
Freud's essay, speaks vaguely of the need for the son to be
delivered from the influence of the mother as well as from the
authority of the father, but it is Danae to whom he refers in this
connection, not Medusa. The situation is quite different with
regard to the existentialist interpretation. Obviously neither
Cather nor Friar has paralleled it exactly, but I think we can
truthfully say that their use of the symbol is not out of harmony
with the Sartrean view and seems to refer to the same elements
in human experience. Cather in particular gives weight to the
state of being looked-at as well as to the act of looking. Both
suggest that as the result of fascination, the inner self, the self-
as-subject is in some way altered. The individual loses his living self—or is tempted to do so—for the sake of a made self or a
nonhuman self. Sartre has written often of the apparently uni-

versal desire (irrational but understandable) to fix the self into a
hard steadfast entity—like a stone—so that one might be what
one is, forever, instead of having continuously to pursue the
self as a freely existing self-making creature must. In a striking
illustration, he tells us that a person who is suffering may look
upon a statue of "Grief" and see in it a kind of reproach. The
pure intensity of the represented pain of the statue is in sharp
contrast to his own divided and, to some extent, freely sustained wretchedness. He "suffers from not suffering enough."[29]
The neurotic desire to identify one's being with a petrified self
beyond the reach of the Other and the preference for art over
life are not entirely disconnected. Friar's symbolism lends itself less easily to the existentialist view, but we may at least say
that for him Medusa's Look, if encountered directly, would
result in the sacrifice of the individual to universal form.

In a number of philosophical contexts we encounter the
notion that one of the motives or meanings of art is to impose
form upon the flux of experience, to capture the universal in a
unique object, to fix once and for all the essence of the ever-
changing existent. John Dewey, in particular, has insisted that
the artistic impulse is not unrelated to the universal wish to
isolate certain parts of our individual experience so as to give
to them the quality of a finished product, something which can
be looked at and appraised for itself as it stands apart from the
unending continuum of means and ends. In this connection I
am irresistibly drawn to make reference to a game which I
played as a child, one which my companions and I did not
invent but received as part of that amorphous heritage of activities which includes "hide-and-seek" and "follow-the-
leader" and other imitations in play of what adults perform as
part of the serious business of living. Our game was called
"Statue." One person, privileged or chosen by lot, grasped each
of the others in turn by the right hand and swung him or her, at
both their arms' length, violently around in a circle. The point
was to freeze in the position in which one landed and hold the
pose until the swinger could judge the group of "statues" and
select the best. The chosen one in turn became the swinger. I
can still recall the anxious but pleasurable fleeting moment in

29. Sartre, *Being and Nothingness*, p. 141.

which we would have to choose and arrange our expressions so as to fit a pose which might be selected because it was the most beautiful, the most tragic, or the most grotesque. I do not claim that this game was created by a far distant child whose parent had told him the story of Medusa—not any more than I believe that Little Orphan Annie recognized in her goblin a descendant of the Greek Gorgo. I do hold that the fear of being made an object by the Other's Look and the impulse to objectify ourselves so as to lay claim to an absolute being and value which the Other must recognize are two sides of the same coin.

A recent and quite extraordinary literary treatment of the story of Perseus and Medusa is John Barth's "Perseid." This is a novella which stands second in a trilogy of retold myths called *Chimera*. The structure of *Chimera* is extremely complex. Time periods are confused by the introduction of deliberate anachronisms and self-conscious intrusions by the author speaking in his own person. Barth reveals not only his thorough knowledge of the original mythical material (*The Arabian Nights* for "Dunyazadiad" and classical sources for "Perseid" and "Bellerophoniad") but also his acquaintance with critical interpretations. We can easily see, for example, the influence of Neumann and possibly Slater, too, when Barth has the forty-year-old Perseus exclaim, "With half a life to go, I felt fettered and coffered as ever by Danaë's womb, the brassbound chest, Polydectes' tasks." Still more pointed is Andromeda's impatient outburst to Perseus. "Danaë, Daneë! You should have married your mother."[30] There is perhaps a sly thrust at Freud and Ferenczi in Perseus's statement that he first realized Andromeda to be woman and not statue when the sea breeze ruffled her pubic hair. In fact Perseus himself (the narration is in his first person) comments on the superabundance of hair in the story. He finds himself tempted to scribble in the sand, "I love Andromedusa." His fluctuations between heroic potency and impotence are a major motif of the story. We have every reason to assume his knowledge of Sartre as well. But Barth's exuberant and wildly imaginative reconstruction and extension of the myth is emphatically not an attempt to give flesh

30. John Barth, *Chimera* (New York: Random House, 1972), pp. 71 and 78.

and blood to any systematic scholarly interpretation of mythical symbols—not even his own.

The narrative structure of "Perseid" is extremely intricate. At the beginning the action is seen to unfold in a spiral with patterns repeated with variations at higher levels. Gradually the reader realizes that the narrative is presented in the form of reported conversations and reflected images. At first Perseus seems simply to be telling us directly about his conversation and erotic play with the attractive Calyxa, whom he has met in Heaven after his death. Calyxa is both the priestess of the deified hero and—as emerges much later—the Egyptian girl who formerly had written to him probing letters asking for information about details connected with the killing of Medusa. She shows to Perseus one by one the panels of a mural, carved in relief, which record the events of his life. Commenting on these representations, Perseus reconstructs the familiar story and then starts on the new series of episodes which began twenty years later. Bored with Andromeda and the humdrum routine of running a kingdom, Perseus found that he had outlived his myth. He no longer coincided with his image. "I became convinced I was petrifying, and asked my doctor if it mightn't be the late effects of radiation from Medusa" (p. 71). Perseus decided to retrace his early career in the hope that by rediscovering his earlier self, he could become the heroic Perseus once again. The improbable dream became a real possibility when he heard rumors of a new Medusa. Athena in pity had revived the Gorgon, restored her beautiful hair and—so went the report—altered the fatal Look so that now it would rejuvenate anyone who met it. Perseus resolved to kill Medusa once again, first encountering her glance so that he might be renewed as the young hero he once was. The futility of Perseus's wish to be identified with his image is expressed by Barth through Calyxa when she asks, "How can Being Perseus Again be your goal when you have to be Perseus to reach it?" (p. 100). Nevertheless Perseus set out to relive the past, which he did—with disconcerting and unwelcome variations. He met Medusa in Athena's temple where he went "to learn about life from art" by examining the Gorgons who were carved in relief on the temple mural—and represented on the

mural shown to Perseus by Calyxa. Perseus did not recognize
Medusa in the hooded stranger in the temple, but he learned
from her the truth about the past and present of the Gorgon.
When Medusa turned her face toward the young Perseus advancing with his sword, she had been offering her face for his
kiss, not meaning to destroy him. Now she was restored to life
by the goddess but under heavy restrictions.

At about this point in the narrative, we become aware of the
presence of a third character, the person to whom Perseus has
been telling the tale of his adventures and repeating the fram-
ing conversation with Calyxa. Slowly we begin to realize that
the unseen addressee is Medusa; she herself occasionally inter-
rupts the succeeding account with comments. We discover that
the scene with Calyxa has not after all been laid in Heaven but
was only an earthly interlude between Perseus's incomplete
encounter with the hooded Medusa and his final direct confrontation. At the time of her resurrection by Athena, Medusa
was told that her renascence as a beautiful girl was accompanied by three conditions: first, if she should ever look at her
own reflected image, she would see not a girl, but a Gorgon;
second, if she looked at anyone and allowed herself to be
looked at unveiled, she was empowered either to petrify or to
rejuvenate the beholder, but she herself would be "re-
Gorgoned." The third condition was an escape clause for the
second. "If the man who uncowled her, and on whom she laid
her one-shot grace, were her true lover, the two of them would
turn ageless as the stars and be together forever" (p. 107). Until
she had seen her own reflection, Medusa could not be sure that
Athena had in truth deGorgoned her; therefore the one who
looked at her would risk being irrevocably petrified. Perseus
spent a week making love to the hooded Medusa, but he did not
have sufficient confidence in his love for her to look at her eyes.
It was then that Medusa had brought him to Calyxa and had
personally directed the carving of the biographical panels.

After more adventures revisiting the sites where he had
gone after the original decapitation, Perseus realized that
neither Calyxa nor Andromeda was his true love. He returned
to Medusa, kissed her, and gazed into her open eyes. For centuries the two, side by side as constellations in the skies, have

been retelling their stories. Medusa says that she is still tormented by the thought that perhaps Perseus's decision to look
directly at her was "an act not of love but of suicide, or a
desperate impulse to immortality-by-petrifaction." What she
saw when she looked at her reflection in his eyes was a Gorgon,
as Athena had foretold. Perseus assures her that he beheld in
her eyes "two things in instantaneous succession." First, he
saw himself as he was—no longer a hero but still vigorous and
"grown too wise to wish his time turned back." Second "was
the stars in your own eyes, reflected from mine and rereflected
to infinity—stars of a quite miraculous, yes blinding love,
which transfigured everything in view" (p. 133).

Even from this oversimplified summary of Barth's invo-
luted and complicated story, we can see that the symbolism is
working on at least two levels. Barth is exploring the
psychological and emotional implications of the Look of the
Gorgon; he is equally concerned with its symbolic possibilities
in relation to the enterprise of the artist. Perseus's visit to the
temple with the carved Gorgons, the biographical murals, the
emphasis on repeated narrative patterns, and the question of
the relation between the flesh and blood individual and the
legend of the hero which he has created but which in turn
molds his future existence—all emphasize the contrast, sometimes even the conflict, between the continuous free flow of life
and the fixed forms which human imagination has imposed
upon it. Perseus's final choice, though not the suicidal decision
which Medusa feared, is in its own way a choice of immortality
by petrification, the kind of eternity which we assign to works
of art. High in the heavens, Perseus still cannot look at Medusa
directly; he can only see and feel the stray strands of her beautiful hair. But he says,

> I'm content. So with this issue, our net estate: to have become,
> like the noted music of our tongue, these silent, visible signs; to
> be the tale I tell to those with eyes to see and understanding to
> interpret; to raise you up forever and know that our story will
> never be cut off, but nightly rehearsed as long as men and
> women read the stars . . . I'm content. [Pp. 133–34]

This passage, if taken by itself, might seem to say that
Perseus's (if not Barth's) ultimate preference was in fact for the

enduring sublimation of art and not for the fulfillment of ephemeral mortal love. This conclusion is denied by the lovers' description of what they saw in the images in each other's eyes. Medusa first sees herself as a gorgon, Perseus sees a middle-aged nonheroic man. But in the blinding interchange of reflections which follows, everything is altered. The Look of Love is not an escape into fantasy nor the neurotic exploitation of the Other which Laing's poem so devastatingly analyzed. This Look reveals, accepts, and transfigures. It is as though Barth were saying that the confident and trusting exchange signified by the Look in love is itself a taste of immortality.

It would be desirable to conclude our pursuit of the Medusa symbol by turning from the consideration of the explicit use of the Gorgon myth to the examination of literary treatments of the experience symbolized, where the imagery is not present. It would be extremely interesting then to evaluate our findings in the light of the psychoanalytic and existentialist interpretations respectively. But aside from the magnitude of the task, we meet an insurmountable difficulty. If we accept the psycho-analytical interpretation (or its Jungian variant), we are bound to accept, too, the hermeneutic method of psychoanalysis. This means that an appeal to literature cannot validate or invalidate the thesis that the sight of the mother's genitals invokes horror and the fear of castration so commonly that we may justifiably assume it to be a universal fear giving rise to a wealth of ap-propriate symbols. Even were we to establish that no signifi-cant account of such an experience existed, we should be told that this was exactly to be expected. The emotion is so deeply repressed in the unconscious that it is never manifested except under the same sort of heavy disguise which cloaks the hidden meaning of the Perseus-Medusa story. Thus we must assume in advance the meaning of the symbol in question.

Up to a point I must admit the logic of this argument, but I am not totally convinced of its cogency. In the case of the Oedipus and Electra complexes, for example, we are dealing with repressed material, but the experience which they repres-ent has appeared overtly in myths all over the world and has furnished material for writers of fiction for centuries. Sophocles' *Oedipus the King* and O'Neill's *Mourning Becomes Electra* are probably the most famous examples of pre- and post-Freudian treatments. Euripides was very much aware that the emotional involvements of the members of Agamemnon's family were an exaggeration of common, if not universal patterns of behavior.[31] The many myths relating conflicts between patriarchal heroes and matriarchal mother-goddess types are transparent in their essential meaning. They are paralleled in hundreds of scenes in fiction and in all probability derived from the events of literal history. The degradation of woman in the stories of Pandora and Eve in patriarchal cultures is equally clear in its meaning. By contrast, the tale of Medusa and Perseus, if it really does involve the female genitals and threat of castration, wore a disguise wholly impenetrable until Freud, and it represents an experience almost never expressed in overt terms—at least not in serious literature.

I know of no significant work of fiction in which the child's sight of his mother naked is a major event in his development. Henry Roth's *Call It Sleep* comes close, but it is the small David's awareness that his boy companions have watched his mother bathing which evokes his troubled reaction. This episode illustrates rather that sense of violation by sight to which Sartre has given the name of Actaeon complex.[32] Roth indicates also a vague uneasiness in the boy at signs of his father's and mother's sexuality. At least since Freud, a child's distress at witnessing or hearing about his parents' sexual intercourse is a commonplace in literary portrayals of children's maturation. Even Sartre refers to it fleetingly in his short story "Childhood of a Boss." The only example I know in which it is a central theme is not fiction but Ralph Lindner's study *Rebel without a Cause*. I, for one, have never been convinced that the incident described there explains adequately the complex psychopathic development of the subject of this case history although its author evidently believed that it did.

The mother who, flaunting her own sexuality, overpowers

31. I am thinking especially of Clytemnestra's remark to Electra: "My child, from the time you were born, you adored your father. That's the way it is. Some children prefer the males, and others love their mothers more than the father. I understand and will forgive you" (Euripides, *Electra* 1102–05).

32. Sartre, *Being and Nothingness*, pp. 738–39.

and castrates her son is, of course, encountered very frequently in literature. She ranges from the tender subtlety of Mrs. Morel in Lawrence's *Sons and Lovers* to the monstrous caricature of the mother in Arthur Kopit's *Oh, Dad, Poor Dad! Mama's Hung You in the Closet and I'm Feelin' So Sad*. I question, however, whether the destructiveness of this kind of female is really quite reducible to the castration threat of the female genitals which Freud sees in Medusa. The literary type may well be equated with the destructive side of the dominant Great Mother, but that is a somewhat different thing. One of her most common manifestations is the jealous possessive mother whose protectiveness is a disguise for the resolve never to allow the child to become independent and fully separate from her. It is interesting that even in Kopit's blatant fable, which represents woman as totally possessive and destructive, the crisis is presented in terms amazingly close to the concept of the Sartrean Look. The boy is neither destroyed nor made impotent by the young girl who serves as a double for the monster mother. The climax, which from one point of view is a deliverance, occurs when the preserved body of the boy's dead father suddenly and literally falls upon the bed between him and the girl. One could almost say that the father is the gorgoneion which has counteracted the paralyzing stare of the Medusa mother. From his father's corpse the boy gains the strength to kill the young girl who is the mother's surrogate.

If we turn to the existentialist view, which I claim is the richer and truer interpretation, then I think we may say without exaggeration that the Medusa theme is in the forefront. Sometimes the focus is on the fate of Medusa's victim, sometimes on the apotropaic use of the mask as gorgoneion. Central is the struggle of the individual who tries, or fails, to find himself and to mold his life in the face of those who would tie him to a role not of his own choosing. Confronting such an extreme embarrassment of riches even if we limit ourselves to literature of the present century, I will but mention a few illustrations to suggest something of the range of concern.

As obvious an example as any is a passage from T. S. Eliot's poem, "The Love Song of J. Alfred Prufrock." Eliot's eponymous hero never succeeded in recognizing and following the dictates of an authentic spontaneous Self, but he was acutely aware of how he was looked at by others. We might say that his hyperawareness of his self-for-others was precisely what paralyzed any attempt on his part to change his life or—as Sartre would put it, to "make a new choice of being." The Gorgon stare of his associates classifies and fixes a dead self.

> And I have known the eyes already, known them all—
> The eyes that fix you in a formulated phrase,
> And when I am formulated, sprawling on a pin,
> When I am pinned and wriggling on the wall,
> Then how should I begin
> To spit out all the butt-ends of my days and ways?[33]

In the lines which follow, the Look of the Other is internalized.

> No! I am not Prince Hamlet, nor was meant to be.

Many years later Arthur Miller explored the same idea in *Death of a Salesman* but from the point of view of one who spent a lifetime successfully striving to be only the self-for-others or—as Pirandello had already expressed it—to be "as you desire me." *The Invisible Man* by Ralph Ellison carries the notion of the lost self a step farther. Here the Eye of Society does not petrify but disintegrates, turns into nothingness. Because he is not seen at all, the narrator comes to doubt that he has any concrete existence in the world. His self-for-others is invisible; his potentially free self is starved because there is no Other from whom he can gain sustenance.

The use of the mask either as a protective device or as a means aggressively to stare the other down is a favorite theme of Jean Genet. In *The Blacks* there is no longer any concern for the individual self. The conflict is between hostile groups defined by class and race. Through the device of literal masks, we watch the interplay between oppressors and victims as the looker becomes the looked-at. We should perhaps not be going too far if we said that Alain Robbe-Grillet, throughout his entire career, has been preoccupied with the nature of the Look itself as the agent of perception. The objects which a consciousness perceives and the way in which it "intends" or attends to them are the "truth" of the person. We reach and come to know the

33. T. S. Eliot, *Collected Poems: 1909–1935* (New York: Harcourt, Brace and Co., 1936).

perceiver through his perceptions. But we must be careful not
to destroy the effectiveness of the Medusa symbol by extending
it too far. The essential human ingredient is the two-edged
experience of our being in the world where the Other is always
present, that Other who may petrify my being unless I manage
somehow to neutralize his Look or to overpower it with my
own.

There was no suggestion in antiquity of any way by which
one could meet Medusa's eyes safely. One could attempt to
neutralize the hostile look by wearing a gorgoneion so as to
become more terrifying than the unseen enemy. Or one could
simply run away as Perseus fled from Medusa's angry sisters.
Contemporary literature has sought for ways to transform the
petrifying stare into benign communication or fulfilling par-
ticipation. Writers under the influence of Eastern philosophy,
like Hermann Hesse and Aldous Huxley, have attempted to
solve the problem by dissolving it. Since the individual self is
illusion or unnecessary restriction, the conflict between subject
and object is only the result of choosing to remain on a superfi-
cial level of existence. Potentially all of us may be merged in
a cosmic consciousness which erases all conflict. Tillich, too,
though he tries to avoid the pitfalls of traditional mysticism,
argues that ultimately the split between subject and object is a
false one. God (Being-Itself) is neither up there nor down there
nor outside, but in the depths of the Being of each and every
one of us. If love is the Unconditioned which makes possible
all conditional human love, then Martin Buber's I-thou encounter is possible not only between a personal universal and
me, but among all those beings who inhibit it. I will confess
that for myself, these half-mystic I-thou relations represent a
form of wish fulfillment as archaic as the grammar. Yet as I
have pointed out elsewhere, I do not believe that the Sartrean
Look is necessarily and always a hostile judgment or a petrifying stare.[34] Even on the purely literal level, the Look that binds
two pairs of eyes may be an exchange. Sartre himself has based

34. I have discussed the positive aspects of the Look in two books: in terms
of individuals, in the chapter "Personal Pronouns" in *An Existentialist Ethics*
(New York: Alfred A. Knopf, 1967); in terms of Sartre's concept of the group, in
the chapter "Hell is the Outside World" in *Sartre* (New York: Lippincott, 1973).

his social theory on the conviction that the Look which alien-
ates may be replaced by a mutual looking-at-the-world-together
in a common project. If all Gorgon masks are laid aside, then
theoretically Medusa should cease to be a threat and perhaps
might be transformed into a means of fulfillment. John Barth
was saying something of the sort in his bizarre but occasionally
tender mythical extravaganza. Edward Albee seems to me to
have accomplished this between Martha and George at the end
of that long, long evening in Who's Afraid of Virginia Woolf?

Realistically, however, we should remember that even after
decapitation Medusa's head was deadly. Moments of perfect
communication are as rare as they are precious. Loving com-
munities tend, if unwatched, to harden into rigid institutions of
terror. Little Orphan Annie was grimly correct in warning us
that the Gorgon will get you if you don't watch out! Possibly
the awareness of our common danger is the strongest incentive
to seek a remedy more effective than the gorgoneion. Thom
Gunn has seen in Sartre's myth of the keyhole a compelling
motivation for the initiation of friendship. Since we are all both
watchers and watched, the only lasting solution is to lay aside
the mask and to learn to look without the use of a distorting
lens.

THE CORRIDOR

A separate place between the thought and felt
The empty hotel corridor was dark,
But here the keyhole shone, a meaning spark,
What fires were latent in it! So he knelt.

Now, at the corridor's much lighter end,
A pierglass hung upon the wall and showed,
As by an easily deciphered code,
Dark, door, and man, hooped by a single band.

He squinted through the keyhole, and within
Surveyed an act of love that frank as air
He was too ugly for, or could not dare,
Or at a crucial moment thought a sin.

Pleasure was simple thus; he mastered it.
If once he acted as participant
He would be mastered, the inhabitant
Of someone else's world, mere shred to fit.

He moved himself to get a better look
And then it was he noticed in the glass
Two strange eyes in a fascinated face
That watched him like a picture in a book.

The instant drove simplicity away—
The scene was altered, it depended on
His kneeling, when he rose they were clean gone
The couple in the keyhole; this would stay.

For if the watcher of the watcher shown
There in the distant glass, should be watched too,
Who can be master, free of others; who
Can look around and say he is alone?

Moreover, who can know that what he sees
Is not distorted, that he is not seen
Distorted by pierglass, curved and lean?
Those curious eyes, through him, were linked to these—

These lovers altered in the cornea's bend,
What could he do but leave the keyhole, rise
Holding those eyes as equal in his eyes,
And go, one hand held out, to meet a friend?[35]

35. Thom Gunn, *The Sense of Movement* (London: Faber and Faber, 1957). Reprinted by permission of Faber and Faber Ltd. from *The Sense of Movement*. I am grateful to Patrick Mangan for calling my attention to this poem.

Death and Cocktails:

The Alcestis Theme in Euripides and T. S. Eliot

Since the day that T. S. Eliot first announced to an unsuspecting world that he had based *The Cocktail Party* on Euripides' *Alcestis*, critics have unearthed so many points of resemblance between the two plays that one might well wonder why, for more than a year, the relationship went undetected and had to be brought to light by the author. Eliot himself appears to have been pleased rather than irritated by the obtuseness of his audience. In his Theodore Spencer Memorial Lecture, he stated that in *The Family Reunion* he "should either have stuck closer to Aeschylus or else taken a great deal more liberty with his myth." He resolved to avoid this error in *The Cocktail Party*.

> To begin with, no chorus, and no ghosts. I was still inclined to go to a Greek dramatist for my theme, but I was determined to take this merely as a point of departure, and to conceal the origins so well that nobody would identify them until I pointed them out myself. In this at least I have been successful; for no one of my acquaintance (and no dramatic critics) recognized the source of my story in the *Alcestis* of Euripides. In fact I have had to go into detailed explanation to convince them—I mean, of course, those who were familiar with the plot of that play—of the genuineness of the inspiration. But those who were at first disturbed by the eccentric behaviour of my unknown guest, and his apparently intemperate habits and tendency to burst into song, have found some consolation after I have called their attention to the behaviour of Heracles in Euripides' play.[1]

1. T. S. Eliot, *Poetry and Drama* (Cambridge, Mass.: Harvard University Press, 1951), pp. 38–39. Copyright 1951 by the President and Fellows of Harvard University.

The fact that Eliot chose to comment in particular on the connection between Heracles' drunken scene and the guest's predilection for gin and ribald singing is probably significant and certainly amusing. In the long-sustained debate among scholars as to whether *Alcestis* is formally a tragedy or a satyr-play, it is this same scene with Heracles which has been offered as the one objective and indisputable proof of satyr-play affiliations. Both scenes serve to insert comedy at the heart of serious material; neither is heavily significant as to the play's underlying intention. It is almost as if Eliot deliberately pointed to an obvious but unimportant clue, ironically commending the critics for their perceptiveness while subtly implying that they might be incapable of appreciating deeper relationships.

If we are tempted to read Eliot's statement as an invitation to us to turn detective and search for clues planted for the playwright's private amusement but inessential to the drama, we should remind ourselves that Eliot also speaks of having taken *Alcestis* as the source of his theme and as a point of departure (albeit "merely" so) and that he speaks of the "genuineness of the inspiration" which he found there. Clearly he intends us to believe that the essential meaning of *The Cocktail Party* is in some way affected by his and our awareness of Euripides' play. Yet in view of his drastic alterations in plot and characters, one might be pardoned for wondering why Eliot bothered to link the two together. Does the connection, if factually true, hold any more significance than the relation between *Madame Bovary* and the unfortunate Dr. Delamare, whose story gave Flaubert the inspiration for his novel? I believe that the answer can be found in a few remarks which Eliot made apropos of plays written in verse. In his lecture on "Poetry and Drama," Eliot criticizes the idea that poetry and myth should be used for the purpose of increasing the emotional or aesthetic distance between the characters and the audience. This he equates with pure escapism. Almost sarcastically he says,

> Verse plays, it has been generally held, should either take their
> subject matter from some mythology, or else should be about
> some remote historical period, far enough away from the present
> for the characters not to need to be recognizable as human be-
> ings, and therefore for them to be licensed to talk in verse. [P. 25]

His own intention is precisely opposite. "Then we should not be transported into an artificial world; on the contrary, our own sordid, dreary daily world would be suddenly illuminated and transfigured" (p. 32). And a little later, "I have before my eyes a kind of mirage of the perfection of verse drama, which would be a design of human action and of words, such as to present at once the two aspects of dramatic and of musical order" (p. 43).

Eliot uses mythology as one of a variety of poetic means to achieve the transfiguration of the everyday world. The myth of Alcestis and Euripides' dramatic treatment of it provide the overtones and even part of the harmonic material for the musical order which Eliot seeks in his own drama. *The Cocktail Party* is not at all what it would have been if Eliot had developed the plot without the earlier work in mind. The connection between the two is neither artificial nor superfluous but an essential ingredient for the play's effect upon the audience and for our understanding of its author's intention, especially in the realm of poetic enrichment. I should like to look at the two plays so as to see how this harmonic material functions. But since the interpretation of both has been a subject of debate and since I do not think that the depths of either have been explored to their utmost limit, I should like first to speak of each one separately and then of their relation to one another.

Alcestis (438 B.C.)

Plot Summary

Apollo, in an explanatory prologue typical of Euripides, obligingly tells us enough of past and future events so that we know just where we are in the story. He says that on an earlier occasion when he had killed the Cyclopes, Zeus's blacksmiths, Zeus had punished him by sending him to spend a period of time in servitude to a mortal. He became a shepherd for Admetus, who treated him with kind hospitality, not taking advantage of the opportunity to treat a god arrogantly. In gratitude Apollo had managed to cheat the Fates so as to wring from them the concession that Admetus might escape his appointed death if someone could be found willing to die in his place. Admetus's parents had rejected this opportunity, but his wife Alcestis consented. Today she must die. Death suddenly appears and accuses Apollo of trying to cheat him of Alcestis too. Finding that persuasion will not work, Apollo prophesies that someone else will come to save her, and both gods leave the stage. Now Alcestis is carried out for her last sight of sunlight. She bids farewell to husband and children and dies. As Admetus is engaged in making preparations for the funeral, he receives Heracles, who drops in for a visit and a night's lodging on his way to accomplish still another labor. Admetus pretends that his mourning clothes are for a remote acquaintance and sends Heracles off to an isolated apartment in the palace. He himself then starts to leave with Alcestis's body and the train of mourners but is interrupted by the arrival of his father with funeral gifts. The two quarrel, and Admetus refuses to let Pheres accompany them, reproaching him for having allowed the young wife to die when he, an old man, might have saved her by sacrificing himself. After Admetus and the Chorus have left the stage, Heracles comes in, ecstatically drunk. He is scolded for his behavior by an indignant servant and informed of the true state of affairs. Contrite and horrified, he rushes to the grave. There, as we learn later, he literally wrestles with Death and forces him to give up Alcestis. Heracles brings her back to Admetus. She is heavily veiled, and Heracles first teases Admetus by pretending that he won the young woman as a prize in a sporting event and asking Admetus to shelter her while Heracles continues his journey. Then he shows Admetus who Alcestis really is. He explains that she is in truth a living woman but that she is not allowed to speak for three days because, as one who had died, she owes this service to the gods of the underworld. Admetus joyfully prepares for a happier life.[2]

Alcestis is unique in Euripides' work. Its happy ending might seem to make it kin to his later romantic plays—such as *Helen* and *Iphigeneia in Tauris*—but it lacks their concern with intrigue and the melodramatic. Mood and tone are more serious, more somber. The solution provided by Heracles certainly resembles that of a *deus ex machina* even though, in strict accuracy, he is a demigod on foot and not a god out of a machine. But this time the ending is not tacked on; it is an

2. I do not think it appropriate here to survey the wealth of scholarly writing on *Alcestis* though I am indicating any specific point which I have learned from others. Critical opinion is divided as to whether or not there is any real development in the character of Admetus. I confess that the change in him seems to me so obvious that I cannot understand how some have failed to see it.

integral part of the plot. The supernatural is not used cynically, as it so often is with Euripides, as though the author were mocking the very deities to whom his characters owe their deliverance. We are not quite in the human world, but it is not the Homeric world either. We cannot know with certainty just what modifications Euripides may have introduced into the original myth.[3] Even the version which he presents to us shows, in its bare outline, connections with a world of folk tale and popular belief which is almost universal rather than specifically Greek. The themes of the queen's self-sacrifice for her husband and the cheating of death are familiar in tales of widely separated cultures. The personification of Death and the dying Alcestis's vision of the boatman Charon, who was himself probably an ancient form of the death god, are on a level of literalness quite uncommon in Greek tragedy. The story of the overcoming of Death and the subsequent resurrection of his victim has affiliations with local rituals which were present in Greek life but derived from practices carried on centuries before the establishment of Greek religion as we know it. Alcestis's three-day silence has its roots in ritual, too. Contamination with death, even a false report that a person had died, constituted a pollution and had to be counteracted by three days of purificatory ceremonies which included the tabu of silence.

This twilight world, so different from the harsh reality with which Euripides surrounds the fallen heroes of the house of Atreus,[4] for example, has been explained by many scholars as due to its position as the fourth in a quartet of plays, the position traditionally held by a satyr-drama. Although Euripides was probably not the first to write a series of four unrelated tragedies, I think it is entirely probable that he may have wanted the last of the plays to offer variety and a change of mood. The three which preceded Alcestis are lost to us, but their titles suggest that they were traditional tragedies;[5] some relief and lightening may have seemed desirable. It would be

3. For discussion of the relation between Alcestis and the myth as told before Euripides, cf. D. J. Conacher, "The Myth and Its Adaptation," in Twentieth Century Interpretations of Euripides' Alcestis, ed. John R. Wilson (Englewood Cliffs, N.J.: Prentice-Hall, 1968), pp. 14–21.

4. Especially Euripides' Electra and Orestes.

5. They were Women of Crete, Alcmaeon in Psophis, and Telephus.

only natural that Euripides' choice of subject matter would have been influenced by the satyr-play. The story of *Alcestis* is not on the surface one which suggests comedy to us. But what little knowledge we have of the satyr-play suggests that frequently it took an intrinsically tragic, or at least epic, situation and more or less burlesqued it. Euripides' *The Cyclops*, the only extant complete satyr-play, deals with cannibalism and treachery. It is surely not beyond the stretch of our imagination to conceive of a dramatic piece in which the sorrow of Admetus and Alcestis would be as nontragic as Nanki-Poo's fear of execution in *The Mikado*. Provide the drunken Heracles with some fellow revelers, stage a rip-roaring wrestling match with Death, develop further the humor of Heracles' hoax on Admetus at the end of the play, and we have all the makings of hilarious farce. At times I can almost convince myself that something like this may have been what Euripides first intended. If so, he abandoned his original intention completely. The *Alcestis* which he wrote is by no means a bona fide satyr-play; it is tragicomedy but not farce. As the play stands, we can detect in it evidence of Euripides' knowledge of the relics of old-fashioned religious beliefs and practices. Concern with the psychology of religion and a certain antiquarian interest in the origin of cult are common in his writing, a phenomenon by no means inconsistent with his inclinations toward atheism. In *Alcestis*, as in all of his plays, what finally dominates is his interest in the purely human possibilities inherent in any situation, however unrealistic it may be as compared with the everyday world. *Alcestis* remains a fairy tale but, like so many fairy tales, it is a parable of human conduct as well.

Sometimes, as in his *Electra* and *Orestes*, Euripides develops the dramatic conflict in terms so realistic that the result is almost a debunking of heroic myth. *Alcestis*, perhaps partly because Euripides leaves his characters so completely within the imaginary world, seems to be rather a genuine exploration of the meaning inherent in the myth. His basic question is the same as always, "What kind of man, what kind of woman would engage in these events which have been recounted to us?" What would their inner reactions have been if we could look into their hearts as they reflected on their acts and the roles which they played? But here the playwright has unexpectedly imposed a limit. His sympathy with Alcestis is very apparent. The entire play is a paean of praise for her. Yet of her own inner life we know almost nothing. He has given her just enough of human vanity, egoism, and weakness to prevent her from being unrealistically stiff or priggish. She shows a bit of self-pity at having to die so young, a trace of resentment that Admetus's parents had been unwilling to allow the younger pair to live out a normal span of life together. She never expresses her love for Admetus in explicit declarations; we comprehend something of its nature, not only by her act of sacrifice, but by her tears as she bids farewell to her marriage bed and by her imploring Admetus not to marry again. Even this request she purportedly asks only so that her children may be spared the possible cruelty of a jealous stepmother, but we may suspect a bit of rationalizing.

Had Euripides been primarily interested in the psychology of Alcestis, his opportunity for a great climactic scene would have been after her return to Admetus at the end of the play. Aside from the problem of the religious tabu, we may imagine other reasons for Euripides' decision not to have her speak. Primarily we may ask, "What could she possibly have said?" To have had Alcestis continue in the same vein as suggested in her death scene, giving a sort of travelogue description of her embarcation in Charon's boat and the sights along the river Styx would be ludicrous. But what other descriptive narration of the process of dying and being brought to life again could be anything but anticlimactic? No matter what heights of metaphor the poet might allot to her, Alcestis's words could only dim the effect of what we may vaguely imagine to have been her real experience. Of course the playwright could have avoided any reference to what happened while Alcestis was in the tomb and concentrated instead on her feelings at being reunited with Admetus. But this would have forced upon Euripides one of two alternatives. He might have written a simple scene of joyful reunion. This would have allowed him, if he had so wished, to let Admetus express his increased appreciation of her and his self-contempt for having allowed her to die for him. These things, however, he had already expressed to the Chorus. More important, the genuineness of such assertions might be a trifle suspect if they came after Alcestis's return when all danger was past. The other possibility would have been to show a change in Alcestis as the result of her realization that she had in truth had the courage to brave death whereas her husband's choice had been for life at her expense. I have always felt that one of the great unwritten works of fiction would be precisely this—to examine the days and weeks after Alcestis's return, during which Admetus would have to prove to his wife that now at last he had grown to be the kind of man who just might possibly be worthy of the sacrifice which she had made for him earlier. Obviously no suggestion of such a possibility was open to Euripides even if a modern reader might wish that he had made his *Alcestis* the first instead of the last in the tetralogy. Alcestis's silence prevails. Unless, of course, we are to say that Eliot has allowed her to break it in *The Cocktail Party.* . . .

In Euripides' play it is not Alcestis who is twice-born in a truly significant sense but rather Admetus. In an early scene with the Chorus, the maid informs the sympathetic neighbors that Admetus will not know what kind of wife he is losing until he has finally lost her. The Greek line is "οὔπω τόδ' οἶδε δεσπότης, πρὶν ἂν πάθῃ" (145). Literally, if inelegantly, we may translate, "The master does not yet know this before he suffers it." The sentence is practically the equivalent of the Aeschylean claim that one must learn through suffering. The painful stages of Admetus's education are clearly delineated.

We first meet Admetus when he bids farewell to his dying wife. He chooses his words so carefully that if we were to judge from these lines alone, we should never suspect that any element of choice was involved. The sun, he says, looks down on two people who have been ill-treated though they have never done anything against the gods to make Alcestis's death justified. He pleads with his wife not to abandon him but to pray to the gods for pity. In view of the fact that it is as the result of a god's favor that Alcestis is voluntarily dying in her husband's place, Admetus's words damn him as a man who not only accepts his wife's sacrifice but evades his own responsibility for what is happening. The very exaggeration of his protests and promises are a voluble cover-up for the fact that he could prevent her death if he chose. He vows that he will have a statue made of her which he will adore and embrace as if it were the living woman—a grotesque idea if we are to take it literally and inexcusable if it is empty talk. In nauseating fashion Admetus boasts of how—if only he had the talents of Orpheus—he would have dared to go down to Hades, how he would prevail against Charon and Cerberus, and would persuade the rulers of the underworld to let him bring Alcestis back to the world of the living. He goes so far as to beg her to take him with her. Alcestis's reply suggests that she was aware of the bitter irony of his plea; she softens the words by using the plural. "We are doing sufficient in dying for your sake" (383). The greatest testimony to Alcestis's generous spirit is perhaps the fact that she helps her husband in his awkward role, recognizing that his love and grief are real even though not as strong as his reluctance to trade places with her.

After her death Admetus immediately busies himself with the funeral preparations and shows more of undisguised egoism when he says, "I shall never bury any dead more dear or better than she. She is worthy of my reverence, for she alone died for my sake!" The scene with his father sets in motion the change in Admetus although his actual words are those of a man totally self-righteous and sure of himself. Pheres is not an evil character. In him we see the devastating portrait of the average person who chooses not to be a hero. There is no law, human or divine, which requires one individual to volunteer to die for another, and this is perhaps as it should be. Pheres lays claim to what David Daube has amusingly yet seriously defined as the right of the nontipper.[6] One is not obliged to be generous beyond the contract. If we find Pheres loathesome in his insistence that even an old man has a right to find his last days sweet and to insist on having as many of them as are coming to him, this is not because he is not technically correct. He holds

6. David Daube has discussed the "nontipper" on two occasions: first, in the section entitled "The Protection of the Non-Tipper," Roman Law: Linguistic, Social and Philosophical Aspects (Edinburgh: At the University Press, 1969), pp. 117–28; second, in an article, "Limitations on Self-Sacrifice in Jewish Law and Tradition," Theology 72, no. 589 (July 1969): 291–304.

up a mirror to the audience, and all of us nonheroes recognize our reflections. In Pheres' eyes, Alcestis is noble but foolish. To argue that we would not ourselves have gone so far as to do what Admetus did does not mean that we would be willing to follow Alcestis's example. Therefore her heroism shines more brightly. Angered by Admetus's statement that he disowns his parents because they were unwilling to save Alcestis, Pheres says exactly what he thinks of his son. For the first time Admetus is forced to recognize that not everybody has taken it for granted that his own precious life must be saved by someone. His father finds him both an egoist and a coward. Admetus sarcastically says to Pheres, "May you live a longer time than Zeus!" (713). His father taunts him by advising him to find many wives to marry so that more might die for him—a practical method of approaching immortality.

Admetus angrily rejects Pheres' charges, but his only defense is counteraccusations. Rather than saying that his wrath blinds him to the truth, we might conclude that he indulges himself in anger at his father in order not to reflect upon the truth of what Pheres is saying. Later in Admetus's interchange with the Chorus after the burial, there are indications that both sides are recalling what the old man had said. Wesley Smith has pointed out that the Chorus's proffered consolation is a not too subtle reference to Pheres.[7] "There was a man of my generation who lost the son in his house, an only child greatly mourned for. But he nevertheless managed to endure the evil, though childless, and well on in life, an old man with white hair" (903–10). If this is indeed a reminder of Pheres, Admetus is repelled by the thought of being like his father. In a concentrated twenty-seven lines, he reveals a sudden insight and change of character unparalleled in Greek tragedy. "Only now do I understand," he says, "ἄρτι μανθάνω" (940). He begins by declaring that contrary to all seeming, he judges Alcestis to be more fortunate than he. She will never feel pain again and has met her end with glory. "But I, who ought not to be alive, who have trespassed beyond my fate I shall go on enduring a life of pain." He sees that he will be unable to bear

7. Wesley D. Smith, "The Ironic Structure in *Alcestis*," in *Twentieth Century Interpretations of Euripides' Alcestis*, p. 42.

his life within a disordered house where children, servants, and everything mourn the lost mistress. If he seeks refuge elsewhere, he will be heartbroken as other men with their wives remind him of his own. Finally, he imagines what others will say of him: "Look at that man, shamefully living because he did not have the courage to die but escaped Hades by giving the woman he married to death. Does he seem to you even to be a man? He hates his parents, but he was not willing to die himself" (955–959).

Some critics—mistakenly in my opinion—see in these lines only a coward's fear of public opinion. Surely this is to miss the point. Admetus had anticipated that he might be reproached by others for entertaining Heracles under the circumstances, but his inner conviction that this was demanded of him as host sustained his decision to do what he deemed right *in his own eyes*—beyond ordinary conventions. If now he cringes at others' judgments, it is because he recognizes that they are just. His bitter final summation and self-judgment makes this clear. "What profit is there for me now in living, friends, since my reputation is evil and my action has been evil" (960–61). Alcestis, who had chosen the gift of life for her husband rather than for herself, maintained wistfully, "Nothing is more precious than life" (301). Admetus in his suffering learns too late the Socratic precept, "It is not life but the good life which counts."

Critics who deny that there is any significant change in Admetus interpret the final scene, in which Heracles persuades him against his will to give shelter to the veiled woman, as a test which Admetus fails. I think this is to misread the evidence. It would be the strongest outrage of hospitality if Admetus were to take Heracles' "prize" for himself. There is nothing in Heracles' words to suggest either that he is not giving the woman as a trust to be protected for him or that he regards Admetus's final acceptance as a betrayal of Alcestis, humorous or otherwise. Admetus's continued reluctance is manifest till the last. When Heracles insists that he reach out and take her by the hand, Admetus still will not look at her and says that he offers her his hand at a distance, "as if I were cutting off the head of the Gorgon." The scene admittedly has its amusing aspects. The trick is typical of Heracles, and the audience certainly feels that Admetus deserves at least this small punishment. It serves, too, to extend the moment of climax by creating a bit of suspense; something of the sort was necessary since Alcestis and Admetus cannot speak with one another. I think there may have been one more reason for Euripides' decision to cloak the delivery of Alcestis to Admetus in the guise of a favor asked by Heracles. It introduces once more the motif of duty to guests. It was Admetus's generous hospitality which originally won Apollo's favor so that the god resolved to save Admetus from death. It was Admetus's reception of Heracles, beyond the strict demands of duty, which made the hero feel that he was under obligation to perform some spectacular service in return. Finally it is in reluctant conformity to a guest's request that Admetus prepares to lead his rescued wife back into her own home. First incredulous, then overwhelmed with joy and gratitude, Admetus sums up in two lines what might well have been the theme of another long scene. "For now we will make our life better than it has been; for I will not deny that I am a lucky man" (1157–58). For once the familiar closing of the Chorus is appropriate.

> Many are the forms of the divine.
> Many things the gods accomplish beyond all expectation.
> That which we expect is not fulfilled;
> The god finds a way for the unexpected.
> Such is the outcome of this event.

Richmond Lattimore, while recognizing that Euripides obviously did not have the Aristotelian tragic formula before him, suggests that *Alcestis* could be read as a deliberate inversion of a typical tragedy.

> If we adopt the admittedly somewhat hypothetical scheme according to which tragedy consists in the destruction or self-destruction of an otherwise great man through some fault or flaw in his character, then *Alcestis* might be viewed as a kind of inverted tragedy. For this hero, otherwise no better than ordinary, has one significant *virtue*, which *saves* him. Thus, again, the progress is from ruin to safety, reversing what might be considered the normal course of tragedy.[8]

8. Richmond Lattimore, "Introduction to Alcestis," in *The Complete Greek Tragedies*, vol. 3, *Euripides* (Chicago: University of Chicago Press, 1959), p. 4.

While unwilling to go quite this far, I agree that Euripides has created in Admetus a mixed character, one who "learns by suffering" as the maid foretold, and who is saved unexpectedly as a reward for this nobility. If his earlier acceptance of Alcestis's sacrifice revealed in him a truly monstrous egoism, his tactfully generous reception of Heracles demonstrated a loyalty to the obligation of hospitality which goes beyond self-consideration.

I do not believe, however, that Euripides is pointing out so simple a moral lesson as I have hitherto implied. He is more iconoclastic. It is significant that the Chorus, while bestowing lavish praise upon Alcestis's loyalty, never seems to question Admetus's conduct. They offer not the faintest suggestion of reproach but accept the assumption that it is not only noble but right for a woman to die for her husband (possibly also that it is right for a subject to give his life for the king). In all probability this was the reaction of many generations of Greeks who heard this story from the time when they were children. Euripides challenged this conventional response. Seen in these terms, Admetus is not a villain but a man far better than the average. In his person, the prevailing male bias of the Athenian citizen is pitilessly exposed. Euripides, in less obvious fashion, antici-pated the attack on the double standard which we find a gener-ation later in Menander's The Arbitration. It is ironic that Aris-tophanes called him a misogynist. He is one of antiquity's rare and great friends of women's liberation!

I think it is the ending of the play which finally makes us feel that Alcestis is not a true tragedy. Heracles' drunken sing-ing is admittedly unusual for the tragic genre, but its very inappropriateness gives it a bitter edge which prevents the ef-fect from being simply funny. The words are not drunken maunderings. Since we all have to die, he argues, and since none of us knows the hour thereof, make the most of the pres-ent day. Drink, cultivate the favors of Aphrodite, and leave the rest to fortune. Being mortal, we should think mortal thoughts. There could hardly be a greater affront to the situation of Ad-metus and Alcestis than this instruction which Heracles pro-claims to the grieving servant. The pair has indeed learned the painful limits of mortality, but Alcestis's death was neither unexpected nor involuntary. Her act demonstrated that a mortal *can* think more than mortal thoughts or, at any rate, that mortality is not to be equated with simple day-to-day existence on an animal level. Service to Aphrodite, for Alcestis, was not sensuality but chosen death. In another way, too, Heracles' words are ironic; almost immediately afterward he sets out to prove that the hero can conquer death itself.

We may note that Euripides has played down rather than exploited the dramatic possibilities for tragedy. He develops absolutely nothing of the serious implications of Heracles' struggle with death. The hero is smugly confident before the conflict and cheerfully complacent afterward. The wrestling match is not even described, and it might as well have been carried on with a merely human ravisher. At best we may call it ritualistic. A happy ending by itself does not prevent a play from being a tragedy. The *Oresteia* concludes with all flags waving. Even *Oedipus at Colonus* records an ultimate triumph rather than defeat. But the conclusion of *Alcestis* does, I believe, prevent us from feeling that a situation has been allowed to proceed to its inevitable tragic outcome. In spite of the fairy-tale setting, Euripides has presented the basic human conflict in entirely realistic terms. Admetus's self-recognition is not the conventionalized reaction of the mythic hero, but the repentant despair of a man of our own world. Yet in real life as we know it, a man who needed to witness the actual burial of his wife in order to learn the truth about her and himself and their relation with one another would not be able to undo the effects of his past errors by any action, let alone find a savior in the guise of houseguest. The tragic vision has given way to the tragicomic.[9]

The Cocktail Party (1949)

Plot Summary

Act One: The scene opens with a cocktail party in the London flat of Edward and Lavinia Chamberlayne. Edward is host. Also present are Celia and Peter, both young and attractive, the scatterbrained Julia, the playboy Alex, and the Unidentified

9. I have discussed *Alcestis* as a tragicomedy more fully in an article, "Greek Tragicomedy," in *Twentieth Century Interpretations of Euripides' Alcestis*, pp. 22–30.

Guest, a stranger to Edward. Edward claims that Lavinia is visiting her sick aunt, but it is quite obvious that she has left him. The Unidentified Guest stays on after the party; in a series of interviews, every one of them comically interrupted, each of the other guests finds an excuse to return, either for a private interview with Edward or to feed him or to keep an eye on him. Through these conversations we are informed of the following: Peter is in love with Celia. He is distressed that she does not return his love and has seemed of late to be drifting far away from him. He asks Edward if he, "as an older man," will talk with Celia about the matter. When Celia comes back, we learn that she and Edward have been having an affair. Edward is as distressed as Celia to realize, with Lavinia's departure, that he really does not want to marry Celia. This is not because he loves Lavinia but because he has never loved anyone. He suddenly sees himself as a middle-aged mediocrity. Left alone with the Unidentified Guest, Edward confesses that Lavinia has left him inexplicably and without warning. The Guest's cynical, tormenting, but penetrating remarks and questions reveal to Edward that he wants her back. "I must find out who she is, to find out who I am."[10] The Guest informs him that he can bring Lavinia back and will do so on condition that Edward ask no questions. On the next day (scene 2) Lavinia returns. Their reunion quickly becomes a quarrel. Lavinia accuses Edward of never thinking of her; he charges her with constantly inventing a personality for him so that he cannot be himself. They can agree only that their life cannot go on as it had been. Edward leaves after Lavinia (as Celia had done earlier) advises him to go see a psychiatrist.

Act Two: We are in the office of a psychiatrist, Sir Henry Harcourt-Reilly (the Unidentified Guest). Alex enters, quite different in manner from what he had been before. He tells Reilly that Edward, on Alex's recommendation, is coming to consult him. When Edward comes in, he is disconcerted to learn the identity of the psychiatrist and still more annoyed when Reilly gives directions to have the next patient sent in—Lavinia. He counsels them together, letting Edward know that Lavinia was aware of his affair with Celia. He reveals also that Lavinia had been Peter's mistress and was greatly upset to realize that he had never really loved her and had now genuinely fallen in

10. T. S. Eliot, *The Cocktail Party* (New York: Harcourt, Brace and Co., 1950), p. 32.

love with Celia. Reilly points out that Edward has tried to hide from himself his inability to love by telling himself that Lavinia was unlovable; Lavinia has attempted to evade the knowledge that she was unlovable by concluding that Edward was incapable of loving. Reilly counsels understanding, compassion, forbearance, and the two depart with the feeling that self-understanding may help them to comprehend and sympathize with one another.

After the Chamberlaynes' departure, Julia (as changed in manner as Alex) tells Reilly that Celia has arrived. The psychiatrist's interview with Celia has overtones of the pastor's study. She confesses that she is overwhelmed with a feeling of solitude and a sense of sin. She realizes that she and Edward were two unreal people using one another. Now she is like a person who has sought a treasure without finding it and she feels "guilty at not having found it." If the search and the remembered ecstasy are all meaningless, she wants to be cured of the craving for what cannot be found and of "the shame of never finding it." Reilly tells her that she must choose between two paths. He can help to reconcile her to the human condition (without the treasure) or he can send her on a more difficult journey toward the possession of what she has sought for in the wrong place. Celia chooses the second path and leaves to make preparations to go to Reilly's sanitarium. Reilly, Julia, and Alex drink champagne together with toasts which suggest the invocations and prayers of religious ritual.

Act Three: Again we are in the Chamberlaynes' flat, and there are obvious preparations for another cocktail party. Edward and Lavinia talk together. They show a warm concern for one another and are looking forward to a chance to be by themselves in a quiet vacation retreat. One by one, all of the other principals arrive except Celia. Alex informs them that on a recent trip to Kinkanja, he had learned news of Celia. As a kind of missionary nurse, she had stayed to look after plague-stricken natives in a Christian village beseiged by a tribe of cannibals. Although it was the custom of the enemy to eat the native Christians, they devised other torments for Europeans. Celia was crucified over an anthill. Horrified and outraged at the news, the company attempts to make some kind of sense out of it. Peter, who had been working for a film company in California, now realizes that his hope of winning Celia by his worldly success did not stem from a love good enough for her but from a disguised egoism. He returns to his work with new insight. The Chamberlaynes decide that every moment is a new beginning and that life is "just keeping on." The psychiatric trio goes off to another party. The Chamberlaynes proceed to greet the first guest at their own cocktail party.

When it was produced in 1949, *The Cocktail Party*, despite its Greek affiliations and its psychiatric overlay, was quickly identified as a contemporary Christian allegory. Or if that is putting it too strongly, the play is an exploration of the possibilities for the Christian life in our society. Eliot believed that a responsible psychology was potentially a natural ally to Christianity.

> Psychology has very great utility in two ways. It can revive and has already to some extent revived, truths long since known to Christianity, but mostly forgotten and ignored, and it can put them in a form and a language understandable by modern people to whom the language of Christianity is not only dead but undecipherable.[11]

Psychiatry is, of course, the lesser partner, and Eliot is not above making sly thrusts at what he believes to be its weaknesses. In Reilly's consultation with Edward, for example, he points out that a neurotic patient may well make use of the psychiatric consultation to feed his own ego, finally believing himself "cured" when he has simply found himself interesting and important. There are skeptical references also to the traditional appeal to childhood memories and to dreams. When Edward starts to refer to a childhood experience, Reilly says,

> I always begin from the immediate situation
> And then go back as far as I find necessary.
> You see, your memories of childhood—
> I mean, in your present state of mind—
> Would be largely fictitious; and as for your dreams,
> You would produce amazing dreams, to oblige me.
> I could make you dream any kind of dream I suggested,
> And it would only go to flatter your vanity
> With the temporary stimulus of feeling interesting.   [P. 111]

11. Eliot made this statement in a radio talk, "The Search for Moral Sanction," *The Listener* 7, no. 108 (30 March 1932): 446. My attention was first called to the quotation by David E. Jones, *The Plays of T. S. Eliot* (London: Routledge and Kegan Paul, 1960), pp. 145–46.

Granted this passage is more relevant to the popular view of psychoanalysis than to the method of the best of therapists. Still there does seem to remain in Eliot a little of the notion expressed by Dorothy Sayers that, in the final analysis, psychiatry looks to man for its truth and not to God.[12]

The office of Sir Henry Harcourt-Reilly is a thin disguise for the Church. Eliot worried lest the reference be all too transparent and frowned on suggestions for underscoring the symbolism by means of stage properties or other dramatic devices.[13] Verbal clues abound. In the first scene Edward complains that "Nobody likes to be left with a mystery," and he cries out that he needs "more than the greatest doctor." He tells the psychiatrist that his ailment is the "death of the spirit." Reilly dismisses his patients with the words, "Go in peace. Work out your salvation with diligence." The cocktail parties are perhaps a symbol of Communion. Certainly the drinking of champagne in Reilly's office suggests the Eucharist. The accompanying ritual represents the Mass; it contains as well echoes of writings from the mystics and speaks symbolically of the journey of the soul to God. At the time of the play's production, critics remarked with amusement that the only one who lay on the couch in Reilly's office was the psychiatrist himself. I do not think that this was accidental or primarily satiric on Eliot's part. Reilly, Julia, and Alex (the significance of the number three is unmistakable) clearly are the servants of God, the earthly means by which human souls may be saved. At times they come close to standing for the very grace of God. More often they symbolize the ideal Christian fellowship in which the children of God help one another. Particularly in the formal setting of Reilly's office, they form a kind of priesthood.

12. Dorothy Sayers says this in commenting on the sorcerers in canto 20 of Dante's Hell. "Magic today takes many forms, ranging from actual Satanism to attempts at 'conditioning' other people by manipulating their psyches; but even when it uses the legitimate techniques of the scientist or the psychiatrist, it is distinguished from true science by the 'twisted sight,' which looks to self instead of to God for the source and direction of its power" (The Divine Comedy, vol. 1, Hell, p. 199).

13. E. Martin Browne, who directed The Cocktail Party, reports that Eliot avoided all words with specific religious denotations until as late in the play as possible (The Making of T. S. Eliot's Plays [Cambridge: At the University Press, 1969], p. 132). Quotations from this book, copyright 1969, are reprinted by permission of Cambridge University Press.

Eliot makes it clear that as a priest, Reilly may help to guide the saint to pathways which he himself has not trod. He is the vehicle by which grace is conveyed. Looked at in this light, Reilly's recourse to the couch just before his interview with Celia may represent the need for the human servant to have contact with the symbol of his privileged service. Even the song's reference to "One-Eyed Riley" is not incidental. Several critics have pointed out that the reference to a missing eye occurs again when Julia continually loses and searches for her glasses, which can be easily recognized because they have one lens missing. William Arrowsmith claims that Eliot intends an allusion here to the old saying, "In the kingdom of the blind, the one-eyed man is king." More persuasively, I think, D. W. Harding argues that Eliot uses the one-eye symbolism with both Reilly and Julia to show that each needs the other in order to go beyond the partial view to full vision.[14] This interpretation is supported by their conversation when Reilly says to her:

> When I express confidence in anything
> You always raise doubts; when I am apprehensive
> Then you see no reason for anything but confidence.   [P. 148]

On either view, Eliot is stressing the idea that the purely human helper needs something more than his own individual strength and talent.

Without exploring such symbolism in further detail, we may observe that the play, as usually interpreted, deals with the mystery of sainthood—both the becoming of a saint and the effect of the saint's presence on others. The crucified Celia has followed Christ's way to the end of suffering. We see nothing of the process by which she changes from the sensitive society girl to the savior figure who, after her death, is regarded as a saint by the natives among whom she had worked. Eliot's intention was not to explain and describe but rather to emphasize the inexplicability, the mysterious transcendence in this transformation. As for the effect of her life on others, we cannot know, as Reilly points out, how much difference her presence

14. William Arrowsmith, "English Verse Drama II. The Cocktail Party," *Hudson Review* 3, no. 3 (Autumn 1950): 411–30; cf. especially p. 413. D. W. Harding, "Progression of Theme in Eliot's Modern Plays," *Kenyon Review* 18, no. 3 (Summer 1956): 337–60. Jones refers to both Arrowsmith's and Harding's interpretations in *Plays of T. S Eliot*, p. 151.

made to the natives who died with her there; her influence on those who knew her in London is immeasurable. The two paths—hers and that chosen by the Chamberlaynes—are usually taken as symbolizing the radical difference between the saint's way and the life of the ordinary believer.

While accepting the general thrust of the traditional interpretation, I should like to develop an idea which is suggested by the play itself but which has been almost entirely neglected in critical discussion. This is the relation between *The Cocktail Party* and existentialism, which, at the time that the play was written, was still an exciting new discovery in the minds of the reading public, both in England and in America.[15] Although works of Kierkegaard in English had been readily available for a couple of decades, they were only now being made the subject of frequent reference in sophisticated circles. Everyone had heard of Sartre's *Being and Nothingness* though very few had read it. His short stories first appeared in English in 1948. *No Exit*, which enjoyed an enormous box office success, had its Paris première in 1944 but waited till 1947 for its first English translation. Although most philosophers sneered at existentialism, and the public treated it like any other passing fad, the existentialist mood was very much in the air when *The Cocktail Party* was first produced in 1949.

The only explicit connection between the play and existentialism is apropos of *No Exit*, and it is a negative one. E. Martin Browne, the director, reports that at the dress rehearsal, Eliot was sitting just behind him. When the actor repeated Edward's line, "Hell is oneself," Eliot leaned forward and said, "Contre Sartre." Browne adds, "The line, and the whole story of Edward and Lavinia, are his reply to 'Hell is other people' in *Huis Clos*."[16] The knowledge that the playwright was reacting specifically against something is at least a clue to his preoccupations at the time. I contend that there is more of existentialist influ-

15. I do not mean that nobody was aware of a possible connection. As I indicate below, E. Martin Browne knew that Eliot had Sartre in mind. A. G. George devotes a chapter to "Existentialism and Eliot" in *T. S. Eliot: His Mind and Art* (New York: Asia Publishing House, 1962). George, however, is interested only in pointing out common themes and attitudes in general terms and does not relate his findings to *The Cocktail Party* specifically. I know of no critic who has commented on this aspect of the play in the terms which I suggest.

16. Browne, *Making of T. S. Eliot's Plays*, p. 233.

ence than perhaps Eliot himself recognized and that, as so often happens, he has borrowed from the man he attacks.

There is no difficulty in seeing Celia as one who takes the leap in faith, the faith which originates in despair, as Kierkegaard has so carefully described it. Reilly's lines could have been lifted from Kierkegaard directly. In proposing the alternate way to Celia, he says,

> The second is unknown, and so requires faith—
> The kind of faith that issues from despair.   [P. 141]

And what of the first path? Many critics have commented in disappointed tones on the dreary, almost sad resignation of Lavinia's and Edward's destiny. In spite of the couple's concern for one another and their mutual dependency, it seems that they cannot rise above the trivial. He compliments her on her dress, she wonders if he is tired and asks him to sit beside her as she rests. They both look forward to their cocktail party and worry about whether or not it will be successful. Possibly they have gone beyond "Hell is others," but we feel that at best they can offer to each other only a pale consolation for the hell of mediocrity which is themselves. Arrowsmith argues that the fault stems from Eliot's own disillusion with ordinary life. He claims that Eliot himself sets so low a value on everyday reality that in this instance his art has failed to transmute it. You "can't redeem what is unworthy of redemption."[17] If Eliot really intended Lavinia's and Edward's drab existence to represent the life of lay Christians—all except the saints and the priesthood—we must wonder about Eliot's own commitment to Christianity. But perhaps this was not his intention. Possibly the first path is not that of the Christian laity but of those who reject anything which is beyond the human. In short, it is the way of humanism—as it is seen by Eliot obviously; it has nothing in common with Orestes' heroic choice of life "on the far side of despair" in Sartre's *The Flies*. If this is what Eliot meant, then the Chamberlaynes' low-keyed existence is entirely understandable and stands in intentional contrast with the ecstasy and intense suffering of Celia's pilgrimage. It ex-

17. William Arrowsmith, "The Comedy of T. S. Eliot," *English Stage Comedy*, ed. W. K. Wimsatt, Jr. (New York: Columbia University Press, 1955), pp. 148–72. Cf. especially pp. 169–71.

plains, too, why Reilly, although he calls the first alternative
"a good life," nevertheless describes it as routine, contented,
second-best, with tolerance as its greatest virtue. It is the life of

> Two people who know they do not understand each other,
> Breeding children whom they do not understand
> And who will never understand them.   [P. 140]

Without wanting to pursue the discussion to the point of its
becoming either strained or tedious, I should like to indicate
some of the more obvious parallels with existentialist thought.
To begin with, there is the choice between the two paths. I
admit that it is not absolutely necessary to see a connection
with Kierkegaard here. The divided path as the image of moral
choice is ancient. The Greeks in the fifth century B.C. instructed
the young with the parable of Heracles' choice between virtue
and pleasure. The soul's position between the kingdoms of God
and Satan are as old as Christianity. But Reilly's presentation to
Celia is a little different.

> Neither way is better.
> Both ways are necessary. It is also necessary
> To make a choice between them.   [P. 141]

One thinks immediately of Kierkegaard's "Either / Or." But we
can go beyond this. In *Stages on Life's Way* Kierkegaard de-
lineates three types of lives. He does not think of them exactly
as a hierarchy. It is not necessary to traverse all three stages so
as to exhaust each one before advancing to the next. In terms of
authenticity, none is more valid than the other, provided that
the choice of any one of them is made passionately with one's
whole being. At the same time the religious stage is clearly the
highest and constitutes the fullest grasp of reality and the most
complete fulfillment of the person. Furthermore it is the col-
lapse of each of the other orientations which leads one to embrace another, just as ultimate despair opens on to faith. Eliot
presents at least two of these stages, and there are strong hints
of the third.

Celia's religious commitment is made entirely in Kierkegaardian terms (even if not exclusively so). It is a nonrational
choice which seems unintelligible, even absurd, to those who
have never entertained the possibility of making it. Her sense of

sin, of solitude, of the need to atone are far removed from any feeling of disobedience or transgression. Her guilt is awareness of her alienation from transcendent Being, a typical Kierkegaardian notion. Eliot makes reference, too, to the idea which has been particularly emphasized by Paul Tillich—that God is the condition of all human love. Even though Celia came to recognize that there had been self-illusion in her relation with Edward, she believed that perhaps the ecstasy is real, "Although those who experience it may have no reality" (p. 139). She had felt an exaltation of spirit even though now "What, or whom I loved,/ Or what in me was loving, I do not know" (p. 139). Earlier Peter had expressed himself in much the same way to Edward when he said that his love of Celia had given him his "first experience of reality." He asked,

> What is the reality
> Of experience between the unreal people?
> If I can only hold to the memory
> I can bear any future. [P. 47]

If we accept the hypothesis that Eliot had Kierkegaard in mind, then Edward and Lavinia, after their visit to Reilly, must represent the ethical stage. Without appeal to anything beyond the human, they recognize human obligations and mutual compassion. Eliot has not been interested in exploring the possibilities of this stage so much as its limits. Nevertheless, the necessity of involvement with others and concern for them is certainly present.

Reilly mentions only two paths. Kierkegaard's third stage (or the first if we think in terms of progression upward) is the aesthetic. This is characterized by detachment and contemplation. A certain objectivity keeps it from being pure egoistic narcissism; the aesthetic man involves himself with ideas and art and causes rather than with persons. Appreciating potentially all things, even those which are contradictory, he is reluctant to look inward and, in a sense, has no self. I believe that in The Cocktail Party, he is represented by Peter Quilpe. It is significant that on two occasions when one character mentions Peter to another, the response is "Peter who?" He is a novelist who moves on to film production, and there are suggestions

that his work is popular and trivial. Significantly, he explains
to Julia that in casting for his film, he pays attention to appearances only, usually preferring the false seeming to the genuine
reality. The trio attempts to guide his life but regards him as
still unawakened; it is hinted that as the result of Celia's death,
he may come to a new understanding of himself and of more
profound depths of experience.

What challenged Eliot in Sartre's philosophy was the
latter's view of human relations, particularly as it appeared to
be summed up in the line from No Exit—"Hell is others." In his
conversation with the Unidentified Guest, Edward says,

> What is hell? Hell is oneself.
> Hell is alone, the other figures in it
> Merely projections. There is nothing to escape from
> And nothing to escape to. One is always alone.   [P. 98]

That this Hell is not a necessary state is the purport of Reilly's
later talk with Celia in his office.

Reilly.   Both ways avoid the final desolation
          Of solitude in the phantasmal world
          Of imagination, shuffling memories and desires.
Celia.   That is the hell I have been in.
Reilly.   It isn't hell
          Till you become incapable of anything else.   [P. 142]

These passages appear to attack the Sartrean view specifically
on two counts: first, that it is not my relation with the Other
which makes my life Hell but my failure to become involved
with the Other; second, that the ultimate isolation of the individual can be overcome. I do not doubt that Eliot felt that he
and Sartre were absolutely opposed in these respects. So far as
Celia is concerned, there is no question. Through her choice
she completely transcends the human condition as Sartre has
defined it. I do not believe that we can say quite the same for
Edward and Lavinia, whose story, according to Browne, is
Eliot's direct reply to Sartre. It is true that at this time (1949)
Sartre had not yet outlined any positive view of human relations. It was another decade before he stated in the Critique of
Dialectical Reason that the individual might ultimately be
freed of alienation in the group. In the whole of Being and
Nothingness there was only one small footnote to indicate that

human relations in good faith were even possible. No Exit is entirely negative, and Eliot might well argue that the Chamberlaynes' final adjustment to one another was superior to the series of torments which Sartre's trio inflict upon one another for all eternity. Yet I find two reasons for believing that Eliot stays closer to Sartre than his remark and Browne's comment would lead us to suppose.

First, there is the fact that while Edward and Lavinia alleviate their mutual solitude by extending concern and sympathy to one another, Eliot does not seem to mean that they have totally overcome an ultimate isolation. Here we do not need to rely on our subjective response to the humdrum quality of their lives at the end of the play. The point is made beforehand when Reilly describes the life of those who choose the first path and turn their backs on the possibility of finding "the treasure," the transcendent ecstasy. We recall that even as he called it good, he stressed that these people married without understanding one another and bore children who would neither understand them nor be understood by them. Rather than being a refutation of Sartre's position, Eliot's description seems to confirm the view that in the deepest sense one is always alone.

Where Eliot comes so close to Sartre as to make me suspect actual influence is in his portrayal of the illegitimate ways by which people try to escape from this solitude and from any genuine self-confrontation. Reilly says to the Chamberlaynes,

> My patients such as you are the self-deceivers
> Taking infinite pains, exhausting their energy,
> Yet never quite successful.   [P. 119]

Sartre discusses bad faith as a self-deception, a lie to oneself which is never quite successful since the liar and the one lied-to are a single consciousness. Eliot's portrayal of human relations as they are normally lived by the unquestioning is remarkably similar to Sartre's. Edward comes to realize that he had been using Celia in order to improve his own self-image. Celia perceives that she had loved a projection of her own ideal and not Edward himself. Lavinia points out that Peter had followed the same pattern with Celia. In their relation with each other, Lavinia and Edward, in the first act, exemplify perfectly

Sartre's familiar conflict between two subjects, each one trying to make the other into an object. Lavinia complains that Edward is not even aware of her as a personal existence. Edward feels that Lavinia has so completely imposed upon him her own notion of the personality which he should be that when she goes away, he "no longer exists." Everyone is a stranger; one is even a stranger to oneself. The Unidentified Guest tells Edward:

> Ah, but we die to each other daily.
> What we know of other people
> Is only our memory of the moments
> During which we knew them. And they have changed since then.

> [Pp. 71–72)]

These last lines are parallel to Sartre's view that the individual consciousness is not entity but process, that a person is a project of perpetual self-making. That is one of the reasons why it is impossible for us once and for all to be ourselves and why it is a futile and self-contradictory hope to know, once and for all, what we or other people *are*.[18]

I do not claim that these lines or the preceding patterns of exploitation, self-evasion, and alienation, either in detail or in the total picture, should be thought of as derived solely from Sartre. All is quite consistent with Eliot's outlook as presented in the rest of his writing. Nevertheless their particular combination in this play and the choice of language seem to me to testify to Eliot's immediate concern with Sartre and not to be coincidental. The matter of seeing human relations as a battle of subjects and objects is especially pertinent. As early as "The Love Song of J. Alfred Prufrock" (1917) Eliot had expressed the

18. The parallels are even more obvious in the first draft of the play, which Browne describes as "apt to indulge in argument, hypothesis, generalized philosophical reflection." For example, Edward says to Peter,

> We only know
> About ourselves, the feeling of the moment
> And that is not knowledge.

And the Unidentified Guest says to Edward, "We identify ourselves / With our action, and are lost when we do not act." Whether coincidental or not, this last sentence is amazingly close to Sartre's claim that the individual makes himself by his acts. Browne, *Making of T. S. Eliot's Plays*, pp. 190–95.

feeling of being made an object by another, in the line, "The eyes that fix you in a formulated phrase." The same poem suggested still more of the feeling of a person's becoming a thing, in an image in the opening stanza.

> When the evening is spread out against the sky
> Like a patient etherised upon a table . . . .

More than thirty years later Eliot uses the same comparison —the patient undergoing surgery—in an expanded form and in a context almost pedantic. Edward's guest says that he understands Edward's doubt of his own existence now that Lavinia has left. It is "a loss of personality" owing to his having lost touch with the person he thought he was.

> You're suddenly reduced to the status of an object—
> A living object, but no longer a person.
> It's always happening, because one is an object
> As well as a person.

The Guest goes on to say that one may "have the experience of being an object" if he is jolted by the unexpected step at the bottom of a staircase.

> Or, take a surgical operation.
> In consultation with the doctor and the surgeon,
> In going to bed in the nursing home,
> In talking to the matron, you are still the subject,
> The centre of reality. But, stretched on the table,
> You are a piece of furniture in a repair shop
> For those who surround you, the masked actors.   [P. 30]

The interplay of the subject and object sides of oneself is at the core of Sartre's theory of human relations and of one's relation to oneself. Obviously I do not suggest that Eliot's use of Sartrean language means that he has adopted Sartre's position *in toto*, not even for purposes of this play and with the idea of attacking it. I do believe that his interest in Sartre's theory led him to adopt some of Sartre's phraseology and to seek to make use of certain existentialist insights, positively as well as negatively.

There are other parallels too, though once again I wish to stress that they are things which Eliot would have found harmonious with the outlook which he himself had maintained for years. For example, though Eliot does not actually use the words "bad faith" and "inauthenticity," the earlier life of the Chamberlaynes could obviously be described in these terms. Lavinia tried to model herself and Edward after society's model of the successful young host and hostess. When she expresses her wonder that Edward could ever have thought himself to be in love with her, he tells her,

> Everybody told me that I was;
> And they told me how well suited we were.   [P. 97]

Their idea of themselves came from the outside. They tried to become what they thought other people saw them as being. Even Edward's awakening to what he has become is accomplished by "The change that comes / From seeing oneself through the eyes of other people" (p. 95). It is notable that he feels even now that he must be, for himself, the man he is seen to be by others.

Another theme to which Eliot gives new emphasis in this play is both the freedom and the necessity of choice. We must confront squarely the either / or of the two paths. But more than that, we must recognize our responsibility for all the nonchosen consequences of the free acts which we have committed earlier. Yet we must not let the past become wholly determining. Reilly comes close to Sartre's statement that "we remake our past" when he tells Lavinia:

> You will have to live with these memories and make them
> Into something new. Only by acceptance
> Of the past will you alter its meaning.   [P. 186]

The words may recall Sartre's Orestes, who refuses to show remorse for his crime but, by accepting it, makes it into a means of deliverance for the people of Argos.

Eliot introduces one idea toward the end of the play which, at first thought, appears to contradict not only Sartrean ideas but any hypothesis of human freedom. Lavinia observes that Reilly showed no surprise or horror at the news of Celia's death by torture. Reilly explains that when he first met Celia, he saw behind her an image of a Celia whose face bore the expression of one who had just died a violent death. He concluded that she was a woman under a death sentence. "That was her destiny."

This sounds like the strictest kind of predestination. As Reilly continues, he modifies the idea of a predetermining Fate

> The only question
> Then was, what sort of death? I could not know;
> Because it was for her to choose the way of life
> To lead to death, and, without knowing the end
> Yet choose the form of death. We know the death she chose.

Eliot offers us here a curious blend of ideas. On the one hand, he seems to be saying that an individual freely shapes the significance of the events he encounters even though they are bound up with happenings beyond his control. To say that Celia had the death she chose is very close to Sartre. I am reminded of its near equivalent in Sartre's statement about Baudelaire—that he had the life he deserved. On the other hand, the notion of prescience, even in this limited sense, is not quite Christian. I suspect that Eliot introduced it because of his constant awareness of Euripides' play. There, of course, Apollo foretells both Alcestis's death and deliverance. I believe that in introducing the aura of the supernatural at this point just before the play's conclusion, Eliot is both underscoring the notion of a watchful Providence above the human guardians (the trio) and sounding overtones of the Greek myth.

The Cocktail Party has generally been taken as a comedy although one perceptive critic has called it a "comedy with tragic relief."[19] I myself contend that we might more accurately say that, like the *Alcestis*, the play is tragicomedy. It offers us a double vision which is neither wholly comic or wholly tragic, nor a harmonious blend of the two, but rather both at once and side by side. The material intrinsically falls somewhere in between comedy and tragedy. Cannibalism is at once too horrible for the one and too grotesque for the other.[20] The same might be said for crucifixion over an anthill, especially when it is reported amidst preparations for a cocktail party. It is difficult for

19. Robert B. Heilman attributes this *mot* to his student Dimiter Gotseff ("*Alcestis* and *The Cocktail Party*," in *Twentieth Century Interpretations of Euripides' Alcestis*, p. 99).

20. I have wondered whether the idea of cannibalism may have been suggested to Eliot by the fact that our only extant complete satyr-play, Euripides' *The Cyclops*, deals with this theme.

the reader of spectator not to agree with Edward's impulsive protest against the waste of it all, and his sense of outrage that Celia should endure such suffering "just for a handful of plague-stricken natives / Who would have died anyway" (p. 175). Although Reilly claims that Celia's death was a triumph, we can hardly call it a happy ending of the kind we are accustomed to in comedy. Certainly there is no comfortable assertion that all is right with the world, that now that this particular aberration is straightened out, we can return to a reasssuring normality. We might just possibly say this about the Chamberlaynes as the curtain goes down. Are we to conclude that Eliot has offered to us a tragicomedy in which one plot line proceeds along comic lines and the other along tragic? I do not think that this is quite correct either. Just as the new peace of Edward and Lavinia is too somber and low-keyed for us to be persuaded that it is meaningful happiness, so we may fail to be convinced of the rightness of Celia's sacrifice. Eliot may have felt that the inner experience of sainthood is on principle indescribable, and this may be true. But without some understanding of what the struggle and the final sacrifice meant to Celia, it is hard for us to accept her death as the defeat of the flesh but triumph of the spirit which Reilly pronounces it to be. It is the very ambivalence of the ending, or endings, which I believe gives to the play its tragicomic quality. Celia's choice seems to us to be both heroic and preposterous; that of the Chamberlaynes is sensible and unadmirable. If we accept the idea that tragedy tends to call us away from the norm whereas comedy returns us to it, then clearly in The Cocktail Party, we are left suspended between the two and with no suggestion of a reconciling golden mean.

Eliot and Euripides

In considering the relation between The Cocktail Party and Alcestis, I am struck by the fact that the parallels which are most obvious, those which may be taken as proving the derivation, are relatively unimportant. Objective clues in the later play are suggestive reminiscences rather than guides to interpretation although, insofar as they may evoke our remembrance of Euripides, they have the poetic value of any literary allusion. Among the many critics who have worked at detecting them, Robert B. Heilman is perhaps the most thorough.[21]

The evidence includes both etymological links and parallels in plot. As Heilman demonstrates, Eliot has tied together the main characters by the letters of their names—EDward and ADmetus, HARcourt-Reilly and HERacles. ALCEstis has been split into two woman LAvinia and CElia. The most obvious plot parallels are the following: (1) The action begins on the day when Alcestis dies and when Lavinia leaves Edward. Alcestis has died *for* Admetus. Lavinia chose to die *to* Edward. She says,

> I thought that there might be some way out for you
> If I went away. I thought that if I died
> To you, I who had been only a ghost to you,
> You might be able to find the road back.   [p. 97]

(2) After the wife's departure, both Admetus and Edward feel obliged to entertain guests hospitably though reluctantly. (3) Both Heracles and Harcourt-Reilly arrive uninvited; they drink excessively and burst into song. (4) Both husbands are mildly tormented by the men who will shortly bring their wives back to them. Heracles prolongs Admetus's grief by withholding the identity of the veiled woman and mocks him by callously saying that time and a new marriage will cure his sorrow. Harcourt-Reilly "comforts" the wounded Edward by pointing out how much happier he will be as a bachelor. (5) Although chided by Edward for using exaggerated language, Harcourt-Reilly speaks of bringing Lavinia back from the dead. Heracles, of course, literally rescues Alcestis from Death. (6) Both husbands are instructed to prepare for the period of silence. Alcestis will not be allowed to speak for three days. Lavinia and Edward are told not to ask questions in order that they may not strangle themselves "with knotted memories." (7) Heracles and Harcourt-Reilly are intermediaries who save others. Heilman notes that they are both somewhere between human and divine. This is literally true of Heracles, a demigod, the son of Zeus and the mortal Alcmena; Harcourt-Reilly is God's human servant by whose intervention souls may be saved. (8) Admetus and Edward (and Lavinia too) are forced to undergo

21. Heilman, *"Alcestis* and *The Cocktail Party."*

moral introspection. "Like Admetus, Edward learns that the real issue is not quantity (of life or love), but quality of life (i.e., 'death of the spirit')."[22] This list is not exhaustive; one might extend it by pointing to other probable verbal echoes and details of resemblance. But to do so would be to risk discovering what Eliot himself did not knowingly put there and would not add greatly to our understanding of what is important in either play.

More interesting than the demonstration that Eliot did in fact model The Cocktail Party in part on Alcestis is the question of the nature of the inspiration which he found there. What implications or qualities did he see in Euripides' play which challenged him to write his own imaginative reworking of the ancient myth?

One thing which springs immediately to mind is the peculiar, almost hybrid style of the Greek play. In both dramas, I believe that the tragicomic effect derives partly from the introduction of improbable elements into a plot which might seem to demand a more realistic solution, and partly from a mixture of styles and moods. The song of the drunken Heracles and even the undignified quarrel between Admetus and Pheres are on a level unusual for Greek tragedy. Eliot, of course, goes far beyond Euripides in realism and in deliberate incongruity. Celia's journey to sainthood and her martyrdom are played against an accompaniment of the lightest of flippant cocktail banter. We might expect that Euripides' tragicomic approach would appeal to the poet whose primary mood has often been the ironic, who wrote

> This is the way the world ends
> Not with a bang but a whimper.[23]

But I think there was more than this.

Despite all the scholarly work which has been done on the subject, I believe that critics have overlooked the most significant link between Eliot's intention in The Cocktail Party and what he found in Euripides' Alcestis. The key word is daimon. A daimon (plural, daimones) in Greece was intermediate be-

22. Ibid., p. 102.
23. From "The Hollow Men."

tween human and god. The word might be used simply to designate a person who had one mortal and one immortal parent. It was applied also to nature spirits and other minor deities. Or it might refer to something more abstract—to a philosophical or psychological force or power. Plato, in three famous passages, illustrates all three connotations of this rich term. In the *Apology*, Socrates shifts from one definition of *daimon* to another in an attempt to demonstrate that Meletus has lodged a meaningless and nonsensical accusation. The charge asserted that Socrates did not believe in the true gods (*theoi*) of the state but had introduced new divine forces (daimonia) of his own. Socrates claims that since a daimon is the offspring of a mortal and a god, a person could no more believe in daimones, new or old, without believing in gods than one could believe in the existence of mules but not of horses and asses. Later in the same dialogue, however, Socrates speaks of a little daimon within him, a divine voice which prevents him from undertaking anything which would be harmful or evil. In the *Symposium* Plato says that Love is a daimon because, as that which is between mortal and immortal, it is the nonmortal force in us which urges us toward the contemplation of the divine. In all cases the essential aspect of the daimon is its quality as an intermediary. It is the link between the transient human and the eternal.

Returning to our two plays, we may note that Euripides has introduced a daimon in the character of Heracles. He is a daimon both literally and in the more significant sense of the term. Within a single scene Heracles shows us both aspects of himself. The son of Alcmena gets drunk and advises the servant to live for the pleasures of the moment since all of us must die. Sobered and enlightened, Heracles remembers that he is the son of Zeus. He sets forth to fight Death at the grave and is prepared, if necessary, to descend into the world of the dead and demand her back from the powers below. Through the mediation of Heracles Alcestis returns from the dead and provides the possibility of a spiritual rebirth for Admetus as well. Greek writers have given ample testimony to this twofold nature of Heracles. The Old Comedy shows him as an amiable glutton. Other writers portrayed him as the exemplary youth who chose virtue over vice. Odysseus told his listeners that he had seen the hero's mortal shade in Hades but that the divine part of Heracles had ascended to Olympus. Perhaps Heracles' greatest apotheosis occurred in early Christian times when a representation of him in the act of restoring Alcestis to Admetus was painted on the walls of the catacombs in which the Christians held their secret worship. Here he is not only associated with other Greek saviors and "dying gods" or daimones but paralleled with Christ himself.[24]

Eliot embodies the idea of Heracles as intermediary and savior in Sir Henry Harcourt-Reilly. It was his original intention to suggest that Julia (and by implication her two associates) was a daemon. Here and in several other instances where *daemon* first appeared, Eliot was persuaded by the play's director that the term would simply puzzle a nonclassicist audience.[25] The word which Eliot chose instead was *guardian*. It is Celia who first applies the term to an individual when she says, "Perhaps Julia is my guardian." This is one of the signs of a new awakening in Celia. Up until this moment, Julia has appeared to be only an amusing, slightly malicious, and intruding old woman who, along with Alex, was preventing Celia from having her decisive interview with Edward. A little earlier Celia had referred to Reilly with quite another name. Edward had just told her of Reilly's promise to bring Lavinia back.

Celia.	But why should that man want to bring her back— Unless he is the Devil! I could believe he was.
Edward.	Because I asked him to.
Celia.	Because you asked him to! Then he *must* be the Devil. He must have bewitched you. [Pp. 57–58]

In this passage one might suspect that Eliot was merely playing on the notion of "devil's advocate" since that is precisely what Reilly had been doing. But later Lavinia, in Reilly's office, asks him, "Are you a devil? / Or merely a lunatic practical joker?" (p.117). Clearly Eliot is making some kind of association be-

---

24. Erwin R. Goodenough, "Catacomb Art," *Journal of Biblical Literature* 81, pt. 2 (1962): 113–42.

25. Browne, *Making of T. S. Eliot's Plays*, pp. 184 ff. and p. 200.

tween the two labels. I frankly cannot see any basis for his doing so as long as we stick to the words *guardian* and *devil*. If for *guardian* we substitute Eliot's original choice of *daemon*, the connection becomes clear. Historically the Greek idea of a daimon as a personal protective spirit or alter ego (the Roman *genius*) developed into the Christian concept of the guardian angel.[26] The word itself became in English *demon* or devil. I do not pretend to know just why Eliot wished to suggest that guardians might be mistaken for devils, but I feel certain that he was doing more than indulging in pedantic etymological play. Possibly he wished to stress the difficulty of identifying, either outside or inside the personality, the forces which press respectively for good or evil. Or he may have been indicating that from the point of view of a person unawakened to the Christian life, the servants of God may very well appear to be destructive. It is possible also that he wanted simply to draw attention to the danger inherent in the act of anyone who opens the possibility of a spiritual crisis.

Reilly and his two helpers are certainly Guardians, but they are not the only Guardians. Celia and Edward, in act 1, and the Chamberlaynes with the trio, just before the end of the play, drink a toast "to the Guardians." In both of these contexts something more than particular human individuals is suggested. Divine Providence is implied. Eliot may be referring also to the fellowship of the saints and of the ideal Christian Community on this earth. Still another meaning is introduced in Edward's first conversation with Celia.

> The self that wills—he is a feeble creature;
> He has to come to terms in the end
> With the obstinate, the tougher self; who does not speak,
> Who never talks, who cannot argue;
> And who in some men may be the *guardian*—
> But in men like me, the dull, the implacable,
> The indomitable spirit of mediocrity.   [P. 66]

This use of the word *guardian*, if we may assume that Eliot had his original choice, *daemon*, in mind, is rich in classical over-

26. In the first draft Eliot joined the Greek and Latin terms. Edward refers to the inner self as the one "who in some men may be the *daemon*, the genius" (ibid., p. 184). Eliot's spelling *daemon* is simply a Latinized form of the Greek word.

tones. Heraclitus said, "A man's character is his daimon," meaning that his personality is his fate. Edward's statement is almost a cynical paraphrase of Heraclitus's pronouncement. Plato, in the two Orphic myths which he introduces into the *Phaedo* and again in the *Republic*, uses the word *daimon* to designate a kind of guardian spirit, something very close to a guiding fate, which each soul chooses to accompany it during its subsequent earthly life. Certainly for Eliot (as in Greece) daimones are both internal and external powers. Spiritual awakening may come from within the self, or it may arise through the intervention of an outside agency.[27] Taking the two meanings together, I reject completely the view of those critics who claim that the Guardians are a governing group comparable to the rulers of Plato's Republic.[28] Plato's rulers had enjoyed the full mystic vision of the Good; they were not one-eyed like Reilly and Julia. More important, Eliot's message is not that law should control us and save us from ourselves. The Guardians are protective but as intermediaries who guide but do not dictate our choices. Perhaps after all the true and highest Guardian of *The Cocktail Party* comes close to being Love, the daimon of Plato's *Symposium*. As the upward impulse in humans which leads them to the absolute and divine Beauty of eternal Reality, the daimon Love enriches and elevates even at the lower levels of human life. By implication, Helen Gardner has linked Eliot's Christian thought with the Platonic when she says that the theme of *The Cocktail Party* rests on the distinction between *eros* and *agape*.[29] For Celia, human love fails but not divine love. Such comfort as Lavinia and Edward are able to achieve derives from their purified compassion for one another.

Although I should not like to press the point, I wonder

27. This concept was discussed by Eliot and his director (ibid.).

28. Grover Smith, Jr., *T. S. Eliot's Poetry and Plays* (Chicago: University of Chicago Press, 1956), p. 220. He is quoted approvingly by Jones, *Plays of T. S. Eliot*, p. 149.

29. "*The Cocktail Party* is built on the distinction between passion and love, *eros* and *agape*, and it is possible that de Rougement's description of the organization of the Cathari, an invisible Church within society, may have suggested the handling of the Guardians" (Helen Gardner, "The Comedies of T. S. Eliot," *T. S. Eliot: The Man and His Work*, ed. Allen Tate [New York: Delacorte Press, 1966]), p. 171.

whether Eliot may not have picked up the notion of the Guardians from the lines which conclude *Alcestis*.

> Many are the forms of the divine.
> Many things the gods accomplish beyond all expectation.
> That which we expect is not fulfilled;
> The god finds a way for the unexpected.
> Such is the outcome of this event.

The words which I have translated "forms of the divine" are
μορφαὶ τῶν δαιμονίων. *Daimonion*, the genitive plural, is an
adjective used substantively. We should still be very close to
the Greek if we translated, "Many are the forms of the
daimones." The lines are a commonplace tag in Greek tragedy.
Yet for Eliot, reading and rereading them in his search for creative possibilities for his own "Alcestis," they may indeed have
suggested the idea of a group of persons who would unexpectedly intervene to guide the course of events for the central
characters of the myth. In Euripides' play, the god Apollo and
the daimon Heracles accomplish things beyond expectation.
The Guardians lead Celia to a triumphant death and the Chamberlaynes to a new kind of life which would not otherwise have
been available to any of them.

There is one other use of *daimon* in *Alcestis* which, I am
bold to suggest, may perhaps be the original or, at least, the
most essential core of the inspiration which Eliot found in
Euripides' play. The Chorus, seeking to comfort Admetus after
Alcestis has been buried, says to him,

> Let the tomb of your wife not be looked upon as the grave of the
> dead. But let it be honored as the gods are, an object of worship
> for travelers. And someone turning apart from the winding road,
> will say, "This woman once died for the sake of her husband.
> Now she is a blessed daimon. Hail, O Lady, May you be gracious
> unto me." I say, this is how they will address her. [995–1005]

The Chorus proclaims that Alcestis, through her transcending
courage and loyalty has become a daimon. She is like the dead
heroes, who held for the Greeks a position resembling that of
the saints in the Middle Ages. She is like Heracles, who did not
become a god simply because Zeus was his father. (Heracles
had a great number of half-brothers whom the god did not so
elevate.) He won godhood because of his heroic and near

supernatural exploits and because of the suffering endurance
which they demanded. Just so, the Chorus says, Alcestis's willing journey to death has won for her a more than human destiny. But as it turns out, Alcestis's grave does not become a
place of worship. Alcestis returns to her husband.[30]

Evidently Eliot studied the play and concluded that two
endings were possible—dramatically if not mythically. He
could let Alcestis come back as Euripides did, following the
prevailing version of the myth. In that case, Eliot apparently
wondered like many of the rest of us: What happened after
that? What kind of a life could these two have together when
the wife had felt it necessary to die for (or to) her husband, and
he had allowed her to do so? Eliot answers this question with
the story of Edward and Lavinia. The fact that he has under-
played the dramatic possibilities show that what primarily interested him was the alternative ending, the conclusion which
Euripides had not chosen. On the level of realistic tragedy,
Heracles would not have been able to overcome death. Alcestis
would have died, not as all mortals do, but like the great heroes
and heroines, those who become saints. This imaginary Alcestis becomes Celia. After his report of Celia's death, Alex says:

                                We found that the natives,
     After we'd re-occupied the village
     Had erected a sort of shrine for Celia
     Where they brought offerings of fruits and flowers,
     Fowls, and even sucking pigs.
     They seemed to think that by propitiating Celia,
     They might insure themselves against further misfortune.
     We left *that* problem for the Bishop to wrestle with.

                                                    [Pp. 181–82]

The passage is not out of harmony with Christian practice at
the shrines of saints, especially in the Mediterranean world. It
is exactly in keeping with what we know of Greek worship at

30. Immediately after Alcestis's death the Chorus says that she will be
praised in songs at religious festivals at Sparta and Athens. These words may
possibly imply a reference to Alcestis as a daimon. An earlier version of the
myth says that she actually went down to Hades and was sent up again on the
third day by Persephone. See D. J. Conacher, "The Myth and Its Adaptation,"
pp. 16–19. If we had more information, we might conceivably find that Alcestis
was once much more of a daimon and less a heroic mortal rescued from death
at the last moment.

the wayside tombs of daimones like the heroine Alcestis.

Admetus was profoundly altered by Alcestis's death. The change in Edward is worked out primarily in terms of Lavinia's departure and return. Yet when Alex brings the news of Celia's crucifixion, Edward makes a statement which indicates that her death will not be without spiritual impact upon others.

> If this was right for Celia—
> There must be something else that is terribly wrong,
> And the rest of us are somehow involved in the wrong.
>
> [P. 185]

These lines seem to me to be Eliot's ultimate message to us. Allowing for a totally different context, another problem, I think we may conclude that Euripides was addressing to his audience very much the same conclusion: If you believe that it was right for Alcestis to die, then there is something that is terribly wrong, and you are all involved in the wrong.

Homer and the Meddling Gods

Nietzsche in *The Birth of Tragedy* said of the Greek gods that they "justified human life by living it themselves—the only satisfactory theodicy ever invented."[1] The gods lived the life of mortals in two distinct ways. Totally anthropomorphic, they not only possessed human shape, somewhat glorified to be sure, but behaved in accordance with human needs and emotions. The compulsion to imagine realistically a corporeal body for an immortal being led to an occasional awkward naïveté, apparently even to the vague notion of a divine digestive system. These celestial beings enjoyed and even required nectar and ambrosia for their nourishment, not to mention the smoke from sacrifices; their bodies apparently turned the immortalizing nutriment into ichor which flowed in their veins or, if they were wounded, might gush forth quite painfully. Besides all this, they lived the life of humans in another fashion; much as they might scorn the "creatures of a day," the gods were irresistibly drawn to meddle in mortal affairs, sometimes directly, but more often by pulling strings behind the scene.

Both the anthropomorphism and the divine intervention have been long recognized and much discussed. If I raise the problem again, it is not in the hope of presenting a startlingly original point of view, but because I believe the critical treatments have generally been one-sided and incomplete. Recognition of one truth concerning Homer's attitude toward the gods

1.Friedrich Nietzsche, *The Birth of Tragedy*, trans. Francis Golffing (Garden City, N.Y.: Doubleday, 1956), p. 30.

has blinded scholars to other aspects. In particular, the fact that we first meet the Olympians in the Homeric epics has led some critics to absurd conclusions with regard to the relation of the poet to his material. E. Drerup, for example, writing in the first quarter of this century, observed the obvious fact that matter pertaining to the gods had been molded to fit literary needs and decided that the whole "divine apparatus" was the poet's own invention.[2] Even granting the near infinite scope of Homer's imagination, I find the notion that he simply created Greek mythology out of his own head so preposterous that it requires no further comment. But as recently as 1965, B. C. Dietrich, pointing out correctly that the epic gods do not determine man's human destiny so completely as to remove from him all freedom of action, went on to conclude that divine intervention was not a part of popular belief.[3]

Now it is inconceivable to me that the author of the *Iliad* presented to his audience a religious framework, the essential parts of which were recognized as stemming from his own imagination. It is much more natural to assume that the attitude of the early Greeks was close to that of traditional popular Christianity with regard to miracles and visions. One doesn't really expect them to happen for oneself or one's neighbors, but they occasionally occur somewhere far away and most certainly took place in that favored era when God communicated with man more frequently and more directly. Of course the poet created freely within the over-all framework of belief just as he molded and unified the assorted legends of heroes out of which the epic poems were formed.

Homer confronted a dilemma: He wanted to tell a tale of that age long ago when gods and godlike mortals associated freely with one another. And he realized intuitively that to engage his audience, he must create characters who resembled lifelike men and women, not puppets moved by strings, but behaving like real people. The result of this twofold demand

2. The articles by Drerup appeared in 1913 and 1921. George M. Calhoun refers to him as the proponent of this extreme point of view, in "Homer's Gods—Myth and Märchen," *American Journal of Philology*, no. 237 (January 1939), pp. 1–28.

3. B. C. Dietrich, *Death, Fate, and the Gods* (London: Atheone Press, 1965), p. 299.

may occasionally reveal a slight inconsistency, but for the most part we find a unified approach in which religious belief and literary device are inextricably intertwined. Every literary usage of the divine has its foothold in a specific religious tenet or attitude. Some connection between the way in which the gods are handled in the epics and the nature of the religion of Homer and his audience is obvious and necessary. Clearly the particular quality of the deity believed in will allow certain things and not others. Greek belief, for example, forbade a god to inspire a mortal with the hope of joining him in Heaven, a favorite theme in Christian writing. By contrast, a Christian poet is handicapped by being unable to attribute any but the most noble of emotions to God and his angels. No wonder that Satan, Hell, and the Devils were invented somewhere at the time of the Apocrypha and taken over by the writers of the New Testament. Whatever else we may say about the problem of the origin of Evil under a just, omnipotent Deity, it was certainly an act of beneficence toward writers of fiction.

My intention is to examine in some detail specific ways in which the epic poet adapted popular beliefs to serve a purely literary purpose. I should like to answer fairly comprehensively the simple question: Just what do the gods and goddesses contribute to the *Iliad* and the *Odyssey*? The epics would be unimaginable without them, but precisely what sorts of literary enrichment would be missing?

At the outset I must indicate two restrictions: First, I will be speaking of the gods as they are fully developed in Homer; I am not concerned here with the question of their origin, fascinating as that subject is, nor with echoes of religious evolution. Second, for the purposes of this essay, I am ignoring completely the weighty and sacrosanct Homeric question. Whether the *Iliad* and the *Odyssey* were written by one, two, or several dozen authors, I shall speak simply of Homer. Even if it could be established once and for all that the two epics had separate authors and that certain passages in each poem are interpolations, we should have to admit that the initial pattern of interweaving the divine and the human was set by whoever came first and followed by those who imitated him. Or if even this is too much for some latter-day separatists, I will state that my interest is in the variety of ways in which the presence of the gods has contributed to the epics as we ourselves read them.

Literary Enhancement

What, then, do the gods do for us as we encounter them? First of all, of course, they add to the epic quality. Just why is it that we feel that the Greek expedition against Troy is a cosmic conflict and not one more dismal example of military stupidity and on a petty scale at that? It is because we are effectively prevented from assuming the only point of view which might find it so—that of the detached, objective historian. Partly, this is simply because we see the struggle from the inside, from the myopic but intense and committed view of the individual men and women who are wholly engaged in it. It is also because we look at the war from the divine point of view, almost *sub specie aeternitatis*. In the context of any religion, the idea that a conflict is a Holy War, fought by God's will and under his leadership, may serve, however falsely, to give nobility and meaning both to those who triumph and to those who suffer or die. The Greek gods did not merely approve or will the war. They participated in it in person. It totally engrossed them. All Olympus was split into factions, and one gets the impression that during those years nothing went on there which was separated from military intrigue. Under the aspect of eternity, the Trojan War assumes superhuman importance. Eternal beings take on temporal dimensions.

In addition to the simple fact that the Olympians dignified the struggle by taking part in it, we may note three specific ways in which their presence contributed to the epic quality. First, the gods, despite their anthropomorphism, never wholly lost their character as personifications of forces in Nature. Thus we feel that as the result of Helen's flight with Paris, the physical universe itself is in the throes of conflict. The most obvious illustration is found in the great battle of Achilles when he first comes out to fight after the death of Patroclus. So great was the slaughter by his hand alone that the clear water of the river Xanthos was defiled by the blood and its passage choked by the mass of corpses. Angrily the river god ordered Achilles to desist. When the hero refused and fought on, Xanthos sent a flood which almost destroyed him. Thereupon, at Hera's bidding, Hephaestus, the god of fire, sent flames to quench the water and return the river to its proper course. In this episode, we see anticipated the conflict of opposites which becomes so basic a theme in the work of the early Greek natural philosophers. Another example is the central theme of the *Odyssey*. Poseidon, Odysseus's great enemy, who for so many years prevented the hero's return from Troy, is not only the god who rules the sea; he is the sea itself. And Odysseus must regain his home by going through his opponent's territory with its terrible tempests and untimely calms.

A somewhat less obvious illustration is Hera's seduction of Zeus, an episode in which the anthropomorphic overlay has almost but not quite concealed the original "sacred marriage" or union of fertility deities.[4] The beginning of the narrative, through it concerns the first couple of Olympus, is recounted in a spirit closer to that of human folk tale. Motivated entirely by partiality for the Greeks, who are being dangerously driven back by the Trojans, Hera borrows a magic girdle of desire from Aphrodite and enlists the aid of Sleep in order to remove her husband temporarily from the scene. While Sleep waits perched on a nearby tree, Zeus implores his wife to lie down with him then and there on the top of Mount Ida. As a curious means of persuasion, he recites a catalogue of his former loves, none of whom he desired more than Hera, and swears that he had never before wanted Hera quite so much, not even when they first began to make love behind their parents' backs. Hera objects that it would be a scandalous thing for them to lie together there in the open where one of the immortals might see and gossip about them, and she urges the charms of her snug bedroom back in their own house. Therupon Zeus assures her that he will enfold the two of them in a golden cloud so thick that even the eyes of the sun-god cannot penetrate it.

> . . . the son of Kronos caught his wife in his arms. There
> underneath them the divine earth broke into young, fresh

4. H. J. Rose, *Handbook of Greek Mythology* (New York: E. P. Dutton and Co., 1928), p. 103.

grass, and into dewy clover, crocus and hyacinth
so thick and soft it held the hard gound deep away from them.
There they lay down together and drew about them a golden
wonderful cloud, and from it the glimmering dew descended.[5]

Scholars have recognized in this scene echoes of the old belief
that the union of sky-god and earth goddess not only was the
prototype of all sexual unions but in a sense insured and made
possible the continuance of plant and animal fertility. Looked
at in this light, Zeus's boastful rehearsal of past amorous adventures serves to stress the cyclic and ritualistic aspect of the
religious idea. It is not fanciful to see the golden cloud as the
sunshine in which nature promotes the growth of new life and
in the descending dew the life-giving sperm. I believe, however, that even without such delving into religious origins, the
reader feels that at the conclusion of the episode the poet has
taken us out of the mood of petty intrigue and seduction. The
cloud-enfolded embrace of the divine couple which results in
the growth of new flowers and grass to cover the hitherto bar-
ren earth is a poetic image which speaks for itself.

In these examples Homer reflects the ordinary or everyday
sense of what the gods and goddesses represented in nature.
Occasionally he depicts a deity intervening in a manner which
seems absolutely contrary to nature. At one point Hera compels
the reluctant Sun to hasten his descent into the ocean so that
the Greeks may find respite from the bitter battle. With quite
different intent, Athena thoughtfully lengthens the night of
Odysseus's return so that he and Penelope may have a longer
time for talking, making love, and resting, a gift most appropriate if, as we are told, Odysseus told his wife the whole tale
which precedes this late point in the narrative. In both of these
instances we might conclude that the poet has simply invented, adding an unrealistic detail for artistic embroidery. I
agree these are but a far-off echo of deities as personifications of
natural forces. Nevertheless even here it is probable that Homer
adapted to his own purpose the old story of how the sun had
once altered his course at divine command, a motif which ap-

5. *The Iliad of Homer*, trans. Richmond Lattimore (Chicago: University of
Chicago Press, 1951), bk. 14, ll. 346–51. In this essay extended quotations in
poetry are Lattimore's translation. Commentaries on particular phrases or short
sentences are made on the basis of my own translation.

pears in Hebrew writing as well as in the literature of many other non-Greek peoples.

The gods not only dignify the epic struggle as a whole; they contribute also to the grandeur of individual heroes by becoming their guides and champions. Martin Nilsson has pointed out that Homer has developed in literary terms the inherited belief that the Mycenaean prince was under the special protection of a patron deity.[6] In addition to aligning themselves on the side of either the Greeks or the Trojans, the Olympians had their individual favorites. Odysseus comes first to mind, and there is a particular point of interest in his relation with Athena. Despite the difference in sex, the goddess so closely resembles the hero in character that she seems to be less a patroness than his alter ego. This she tells him in almost so many words when the two meet on the shores of Ithaca. Athena, disguised as a young shepherd, answers Odysseus's inquiries by telling him the name of the island on which he has been placed ashore while sleeping. Odysseus tells her a long yarn hiding his true identity. Thereupon the goddess reveals herself, commends him a bit ironically for his powers of dissimulation. She goes on to say that they are two of a kind.

> You and I both know
> sharp practice, since you are far the best of all mortal
> men for counsel and stories, and I among all the divinities
> am famous for wit and sharpness.[7]

I have been interested to observe that many of my students, who approach Homer without the weight of classical scholarship to guide their response, often misunderstand the divine protection, arguing that apparently great heroes would have been poor weak creatures if left to fight by their own mortal selves. I must acknowledge that the students might find some support for this view in Homer's own words. There are a number of parallels to the cry of the dying Patroclus, protesting that it was Apollo who struck the fatal blow and not Hector. In one amusing incident Homer himself seems almost to laugh at

6. Martin P. Nilsson, *A History of Greek Religion* (New York: Norton, 1964), p. 155.

7. *The Odyssey of Homer*, trans. Richmond Lattimore (New York: Harper and Row, 1965), bk. 12, ll. 296–99.

the "mamma's boy" dependency of his heroes on their foster-
ing deities. At the time of the funeral games to honor Patroclus,
Odysseus is racing with Ajax, son of Oileus, who is slightly
ahead. Odysseus prays to Athena, who makes Ajax slip on
some cow manure. With mingled good humor and irritability,
Ajax says, almost in modern Greek, "O popoi! I was tripped up
by that goddess who has always stood by Odysseus and looked
after him like a mother!"[8] And all the Greeks laugh. But, of
course, as so many critics have pointed out, this way of looking
at things is to miss the point. The gods bestow their favors only
on those who deserve it. ("It takes money to make money!")
The god's protection is itself the mark of honor and recognition
of achievement.

In an article called "The Divine Entourage in Homer," G. M.
Calhoun demonstrates convincingly that at almost every point
where a major hero plays a leading part, a tutelary deity is
present to lend him greater glory.[9] I do not deny that this is
true. Yet this light of the god seems to blind Calhoun to other
functions of the divine presence. Calhoun, for example, sees in
this enhancement of the hero a sufficient explanation for the
presence of the gods at the beginning and the end of the Odyssey. But as I hope to show later, both the arousal of Telemachus
and the encounter with the revenge-hungry families of the
suitors involve a far more significant use of the divine than the
simple device to shed luster on Odysseus's son and father. Still
less can I agree with the extreme statement by G. M. A. Grube,
that divine interventions on behalf of their favorites are nothing but "dramatic and poetic symbols of the greatness of particular heroes."[10]

If Homeric heroes appear more than life-size as the conse-
quence of the gods' favor, we should not overlook the effect of
their sometimes having to confront the deities as opponents.
Despite the constantly reiterated maxim that mortals cannot
fight successfully against the gods, there were occasions in the

8. Homer Iliad 23. 782–83.
9. George M. Calhoun, "The Divine Entourage in Homer," American Journal of Philology, no. 243 (July 1940), pp. 257–77.
10. G. M. A. Grube, "The Divine World of the Odyssey," in Studies in
Honour of Gilbert Norwood, ed. Mary E. White (Toronto: University of Toronto
Press, 1952), pp. 3–19.

Iliad when mortals actually did enter into conflict with them and won. An outstanding instance is the story of Diomedes (book 5), who engages in physical combat with Aphrodite and Ares and actually wounds them. When these two fly weeping to Olympus, Diomedes goes on to fight with Apollo himself, against the explicit warning of Athena, and only desists after being personally rebuked by the god on the fourth try.

Diomedes' face-to-face encounter with the Olympians on the battlefield is in sharp contrast to a comparable scene from the Bhagavad-Gita. The two accounts placed side by side seem to me to encapsulate magnificently the essential difference between Indian and Aryan views of the relation between human and divine reality. In both episodes a god lifts for a brief period the mortal veil from the eyes of the hero so that he can see the scene about him as it really is. Athena shows to Diomedes a battlefield in which the gods are busily engaged in helping their favorites to win. Nothing is changed expect for their revealed physical presence. Now that he can see his adversaries, Diomedes is told to go out to fight them—on exactly the same basis as he would battle with mortals. In the Bhagavad-Gita Krishna allows the hero Arjuna to look beneath the veil of Maya. What he beholds now is not the same landscape with hitherto hidden presences revealed. His is rather a metaphysical vision. He perceives, not with his eyes, but with his spirit, that the battle between the two great families is not a bitter conflict between opposing forces. In truth it has no significance whatsoever, for all distinctions are lost in the eternal oneness of the sole absolute reality. Arjuna is consoled, for he realizes that he no longer has to grieve for the dying. With his heart eased, he reluctantly prepares to return to the world of struggle, but he knows that it is at worst a temporary sojourn, in truth not even a separation from the veiled eternity which enfolds him. To fight in single-hand combat with three divine beings in a battle where all the gods are taking sides—or to be shown that from the point of view of eternity, one is engaged in a conflict that is purely illusory! One could hardly find a sharper contrast.

Along with contributing to the epic quality, the supernatural world makes it possible for us to read many things in the poems symbolically, though never as direct allegory. To what degree the poet himself was fully aware of these layers of meaning we cannot possibly know though I should find it hard to believe that it all came about unconsciously or because he unknowingly handled material into which symbolic meanings were already interwoven. The *Iliad* lends itself less easily to symbolic interpretation than the *Odyssey* though at least two examples are almost blatantly obvious. Ares has become so totally identified with the spirit of battle that his name is often used as the metaphorical equivalent of battle lust. Thus Homer may speak of an individual warrior who "breathes in Ares" or "stirs up Ares" in his heart even though it has been explicitly stated a bit earlier that the god himself is elsewhere on the battlefield, giving courage to people on the other side. The most sustained use of symbol is in the episode following the duel between Menelaus and Paris. Disgusted with her lover's cowardice and possibly reminded of the superior virtue of her former husband, Helen defies Aphrodite who bids her to go to Paris. When the goddess threatens to abandon her to the hatred of both Greeks and Trojans, Helen obeys and goes home. It is Aphrodite who draws up an armchair so that Helen may sit directly facing her lover; it is Paris's seductive words of love which end the lovers' quarrel and induce Helen to let him lead her into the bedroom.

The *Odyssey* reaches beyond itself in its very theme. One may describe it as the epic of man against nature. We may see it as the story of a man who proves himself as hero by undergoing a series of trials and tests. The symbolic aspect is especially clear in the first-person narrative in which Odysseus relates his adventures to his last hosts, the Phaeacians. In this section, which has long been recognized as derived from the world of *Märchen*, folk tale, and fairy tale, every episode may be read as coated with a more or less thin veil of allegory. Some obvious examples: To begin with, there are the Lotus Eaters. It is significant that this encounter takes place early in the narrative. Odysseus and his men have just started on what is evidently going to be a perilous journey to an uncertain end. The men who taste the lotus are blissfully content with material comfort in this strange land here and now. Is it worth it to struggle homeward? Or to put it more meaningfully, why be an epic hero? For those who fail to envision the goal or who find it without value, it is sensible simply to refuse to meet the tests. At the opposite extreme we find the Sirens, who tempt their listeners with the promise of knowledge forbidden to man, an early anticipation of the Faust theme. Scylla and Charybdis may indeed echo mariners' fear of the Strait of Messina. Also they clearly stand for the "Devil and the deep blue sea," the kind of human situation in which no courage or wisdom can enable one to do more than make the best of a bad bargain, salvage what can be saved, and cut one's losses. In Hades the hero must "walk in the valley of death" and put himself in touch with the wisdom of those who have lived before him. And so on. Odysseus is any man (or woman) who is willing to brave all, to face whatever is necessary in the attempt to find his home, his center, his self-realization. The universality of these adventures is so overwhelming that it is not surprising that James Joyce so easily and so marvelously could re-create the experiences of Odysseus and Telemachus in the lives of an Irish Jew and a young artist in Dublin.

A more purely literary contribution of the gods to the Homeric epics is found in their choral function. Partially detached from the mainstream of action and yet deeply concerned about it, the Olympians perform some of the duties later assigned to the tragic chorus. They certainly add to the entertainment value of the poems; I am tempted to say, in Aristotelian terminology, that they contribute to the "spectacle." This they can do for the simple reason that they are not limited to the demands of strict realism and essential connection with the plot, just as the chorus in tragedy was not. They add poetic embellishment and the sense of the marvelous. They comment philosophically on events. They do not, so far as we can tell, present the author's personal point of view although in the *Odyssey* they seem to come close to providing an objective frame for the story. They serve also to tie past, present, and future together. Both in the *Iliad* and in the *Odyssey* Zeus informs us ahead of time how the story is going to come out. It is perhaps significant that already in Homer we see the Greek preference for tragic irony over suspense.

Physical Intervention

The gods, both in their own sphere and insofar as they come
into contact with humans, form a kind of Third World. They
may sometimes resemble officious parents overlooking the
games of children—and interfering with them from time to
time. On other occasions they come dangerously near to behaving like oppressive authorities ruling paternalistically over
their subjects. Homer plays up the ambivalence of these beings
who are in the human world but not of it. To some degree they
remain always on the outside. In fact at times the heroic element is almost threatened by the frequency with which one god
reminds another that the pitiful affairs of wretched mortals are
not worth getting upset about. Yet this remark is most likely to
be offered as a consolation for disappointment or even to smack
of sour grapes. Most of the time the gods are inveterate med-
dlers, and as such they add considerably to plot complexity.
They meddle in a variety of ways, and it may be worth our
while to examine these one by one.

   Frequently the gods engage in direct physical intervention.
This is not necessarily at times of great crisis. Often indeed it is
not strictly for the sake of solving a problem but for the sake of
poetic embroidery. The poet seems to delight in the gratuitous
exercise of the imagination, apparently for no other reason than
to display the marvelous quality of life in the bygone age of
wonders. It is in this context that I would place Ino, who offers
Odysseus a magic, life-sustaining veil and bids him jump with
it into the sea when his own common sense told him it would
be wiser to trust to his raft. We might include here also those
passages in which Athena suddenly makes a man or woman
appear more physically attractive (Penelope to the eyes of the
suitors, Odysseus to Nausicaa and later to Penelope). These
divine activities add much to the way of interest and poetic
enrichment but are not essential to the plot.

   More of a problem are actions of the kind which, later in
tragedy, led Aristotle to introduce into literary criticism the
notion of the *deus ex machina*. It is undeniable that if we take
Homer literally, divine intervention determines a great many
outcomes in which a human life is at stake. There are, first of

all, the numerous miraculous rescues. Calhoun and Grube both have effectively discussed these as a means by which Homer solved a delicate and difficult dilemma.[11] If our interest is to be maintained in the battle scenes, we must see the major figures meet in combat; but there are some whom Homer cannot allow to be killed since they are needed for later parts of the epic. Therefore he takes recourse in showing us duels in which a divine onlooker stops the fight just at the point when his or her favored warrior might have been killed, by literally snatching him away or by bringing in a cloud of dust to separate the fighters, or by some other comparable device. This is all very well, but it raises a serious question. If Homer himself believed, or could expect his audience to believe, that the outcome of combat was thus divinely decided, regardless of the relative strength and skill of the heroes, does this leave us with the feeling that events in the epic are contrived in the pejorative sense of *deus ex machina* or worse that men are mere puppets of supernatural forces? If we examine these escapes and inconclusive duels, we find that there are three types. Let us consider an example of each. First, there is Aeneas's encounter with Achilles. Here Poseidon casts a mist in front of Achilles' eyes and saves the future founder of Rome in the nick of time by lifting him up and throwing him out of range. As Achilles' vision clears, he remarks with surprise that what had earlier seemed ineffectual boasting on Aeneas's part was true: he really was beloved by the immortals.[12] If there were very much of this kind of thing, we might feel that it was in truth a defect in the epic. But Homer is sparing in his use of such obvious rescues. He has other means at his disposal for ending battles prematurely. When Hector and Ajax fight in single combat and neither is able to overcome the other, heralds from both sides stop them with the feeble argument that it is growing dark. Finally, we should consider the duel of Paris and Menelaus in book 3. Paris has been thoroughly beaten by Menelaus, and his death is imminent when Aphrodite, once again using the convenient device of a cloud, snatches him up and sets him down

11. Calhoun, "The Divine Entourage in Homer." Grube, "Divine World of the Odyssey."
12. Homer *Iliad* 20. 344–50.

in his own home. We can see why Homer wished to use divine intervention at this point. As the cuckolded husband, Menelaus could easily become a figure of ridicule or contempt, at best of pity. His dignity and superior merit can be proved only in a public single combat. But Homer cannot have the war end now even though the opposing sides had agreed that it was to be "winner take all." So Paris is saved but ignominiously. It is important to note that whereas the receiver of divine favor is normally esteemed highly for this very reason, Paris is not honored on this occasion. Rather he is considered a weakling and a coward. Even the Trojans, Homer tells us, would not have concealed him from Menelaus for "they hated him like black death." In this episode Homer uses Aphrodite as a technical means for saving Paris but views the rescue as the equivalent of running away.

The inconclusive duel is rare as compared with the vast number of episodes in which one of the pair does die and a god determines who it will be. We may observe, however, that the deity never directly kills anyone either manually or by the power of magic. Some mundane element is always introduced. Divine intervention of this kind seems to me to be not the hand of Fate but the explanation (almost the personification) of Chance. It is the spear that on one occasion hits its mark, on another misses or gets caught in a fold of leather. It is breast-plates that do or do not prevent the point from piercing, weapons that break, helmets whose straps give way. It is the dizziness or the second wind which comes to a warrior at the critical moment. Such divinely explained events are not limited to battles. Odysseus tells us how the gods put him to sleep while his men killed Helios's cattle. (He is willing to take full responsibility himself for sleeping while his sailors opened Aeolus's bag of winds.) Or the god may appear in the guise of the passing stranger, like Athena in the form of the Phaeacian who shouted encouraging words to Odysseus when his morale needed uplifting in the discus-throwing contest. We find a multitude of incidents in which a deity intervenes and almost as many which are described in terms of chance, strength, and skill. The gods are used to explain the eternal "cussedness of things" and sometimes seem to be very little different from the mysterious "luck" which hovers over the players at Las Vegas.

There is, however, one great exception. In the last book of the *Odyssey*, divine intervention prevents the onset of a great battle between Odysseus's family and the relatives of the dead suitors. The lines have been drawn, Laertes has killed one man when Zeus throws a thunderbolt and Athena, not indirectly or in disguise but with a commanding shout from heaven, orders Odysseus to make peace. The epic concludes with the statement that both sides made sworn pledges under the supervision of the goddess in the form of the Ithacan citizen, Mentor. This is a unique example, and one wonders if the author realized the extent to which this occasion of divine interference is radically different from all others. Not only is the command spoken from above to both sides, but it results in behavior which is contrary to established custom and to psychological probability. The author's purpose, of course, is to bring his story to a definite conclusion, not merely to a stop. I believe that we are not going too far if we see here a premonition of Aeschylus, a sense that somehow justice demanded something more than unending blood vengeance. Naturally Homer could not at that stage have formulated the problem in Aeschylean terms, let alone try to solve it. Nevertheless I believe that there is a hint or a hope that there may exist a divine justice after which men should seek to model their conduct and their institutions. If this is going too far, then I should argue that at least the author is expressing in this event his sense of a problem which contemporary human thought could not solve for him and which led him to take recourse in the gods. In so doing, he is beginning to give to the notion of divine intervention a meaning beyond that of the ordinary meddling on the part of the Olympians and consequently to hint at a religious outlook different from what we know as typically Homeric. This interpretation would be in keeping with the established critical view that in the *Odyssey* we see several indications of the belief that gods ought to uphold the best of human ideals and not simply to reflect the dismal pattern of most human behavior.

Psychological Intervention

The gods' meddling is not confined to the manipulation of external events. They are deeply involved with the inner life of man. They make suggestions which today would be treated as forces within the human psyche. In short, they provide psychological motivation.[13] We meet immediately two important problems. First, is the divine counsel psychologically probable so that the human actors do not act out of character? Second, is the gods' activity determining? Or—to put it a little differently—how literally did Homer and the Greeks of his time believe that motivation and decisions were instilled in them from external forces rather than resulting from their own responsible choice?

We may answer the first question easily and emphatically. Homer employs a variety of devices to introduce the divine suggestions. Direct appearance of a deity is rare. Frequent are dreams, the appearance of a god or goddess disguised as relative, friend, or passing stranger; often there is the simple implantation of a thought or an emotion. Without exception the same results could have been achieved naturalistically without divine agency; the resultant behavior is strictly in keeping with the character of the person approached and with the immediate situation. A few illustrations may be helpful.

We may group examples of divine motivation into four types. First and most obviously a god may personify a specific human emotion or mental attitude. We have seen an example of this in Aphrodite's appearance to Helen, where the goddess so clearly stands for erotic love that she becomes almost an allegorical figure. In other passages where Helen uses Aphrodite's pressure as an excuse for her elopement, her words are exactly equivalent to the contemporary statement, "I know that I behaved badly, but I was so in love I couldn't think straight." Ate, the goddess of rashness or blinding anger, is similarly blamed by Agamemnon for his fatal decision to take Briseis away from Achilles. We observed earlier that Ares might fill a man with blood lust on the battlefield. It is not only regrettable emotions which are attributed to divine agency. Athena in particular is given credit for many a sudden bright idea. One of the passages most often referred to in this connection shows her as the sober second thought; this is the episode

13. Credit for the first full discussion of this function of the Homeric gods is generally given to Nilsson, chap. 5, "The Homeric Anthropomorphism and Rationalism," *A History of Greek Religion*.

early in the *Iliad* when she appears, invisible to all except Achilles, holds him back by the hair, and reminds him that it is not a good idea to go around smiting scepter-bearing kings with his sword.

A second situation which is likely to involve a counseling god occurs when an important and fateful decision is made, especially an unwise one. Two examples may illustrate the psychological insight of Homer which lies beneath what is presented as simple intrigue by the Olympians. The first is the famous false Dream sent by Zeus to Agamemnon. Zeus's motive is simply to make sure that the Greeks will launch an attack which will prove disastrous for them in order that he may keep his promise to Achilles' mother and make the Greeks regret the hero's withdrawal. The Dream, assuming the form of Nestor, tells Agamemnon in his sleep that now is the time to take Troy, that all the gods have agreed to support him and the Greeks against the Trojans. Upon awaking, Agamemnon resolves to approach first the other Greek leaders, then the popular assembly so as to test his personal power and, he hopes, lead the troops to victory at last. No sophisticated Freudian approach is needed to interpret this dream. It is pure wish fulfillment. Agamemnon has just confronted a crisis in which his leadership was seriously challenged; in all probability he realizes uneasily that he has acted wrongly, or at least unwisely. What would be more natural for him than to dream that the oldest and most respected of the Greek princes would personally urge him to lead out the troops and would express confidence that Heaven will ensure success. His decision to test his strength with his men and to prove that he can take Troy without Achilles is as understandable as it was rash.

My second example is Pandarus's reckless shooting of the arrow which breaks the truce after Menelaus's defeat of Paris in single combat. Again the initial impulse comes in the form of a motive for the Olympians, this time for Hera and Athena, who want to prevent the Greeks and Trojans from making peace before Troy has been destroyed. Athena, disguised as the Trojan prince Laodokos, points out to Pandarus that this would be the perfect opportunity to kill the unsuspecting Menelaus and that if Pandarus were to do so, he would win honor from all the Trojans and gifts of gratitude from Paris. Pandarus listens to this calculating persuasion and shoots. Whether we assume that he thought up the idea himself or gave in to the evil counsel of a companion, Pandarus's action is all too intelligible in purely human terms. It is likewise understandable that he would tell the Trojans afterward that he would not have committed the action if a god had not so advised him.

Martin Nilsson pointed out that the gods were held responsible for a human act primarily upon occasions when a person wanted to evade blame for an unwise action or when he wondered after the event what ever had "possessed" him to behave in a manner so contrary to his normal reactions. In other words, humans resorted to the notion of divine motivation (not in full, deliberate consciousness, of course) in order to avoid facing up to the consequences of their own responsibility. Without precisely disagreeing with Nilsson, I think that the issue is more complex. We have seen that the gods might be credited with good counsel as well as bad. It would be more accurate to say that the Greeks projected upon supernatural forces aspects of the personality which even today we find difficulty in comprehending. Just as the gods represented little understood forces of nature, so they served to explain the mysteries of the human psyche.

Homer uses the gods in connection with two other psychological phenomena which do not quite fit under the heading of either emotional and mental states or sudden decisions. One of these is the process of psychological maturation. There are two examples in the Odyssey which are developed in some detail and with great sensitivity. The first is the case of Telemachus. Odysseus's son is just ready to step over the threshold into adulthood, but he himself is not aware of the fact. For years he has been the young boy, observing in passive indignation the depredations of the suitors, childishly irritated with the ineffectual conduct of his mother but with no idea of ever asserting himself against her. Athena, disguised as a visiting stranger, Mentes, awakens Telemachus to the thought that he is now a man by treating him as one. You ought to do something, she says. And Telemachus responds by following through with all of her suggestions. He challenges the suitors, instructs his mother to return to her own apartment while he takes care of what needs to be done, and sets out on a voyage to track down information about his father. Remarkably similar, though by no means an obvious repetition, is the treatment of Nausicaa in book 6. On the surface, the only reason for Athena's intervention here is the wish to bring Nausicaa down to the seashore as a safe person to receive the shipwrecked Odysseus. Obviously Homer could have accomplished this simply by having the princess appear there, hardly an unusual event on an island so small that the women of the royal family supervised the household laundry at the water's edge. Instead he has sketched in some detail the girl's progress from child to woman, making her awakening coincide with Odysseus's arrival in such a way that it is both responsible for her receiving him as she did and furthered by this first encounter with a male stranger from faraway parts of the world. This time Athena appears in a dream, taking on the form of one of Nausicaa's girl friends. In a manner which would have been perfectly natural in daytime conversation, she reminds the princess that she is a young lady now and of marriageable age. If she is to show to the adults that she is indeed grown-up, she must assume her share of household duties. What better way than to go on an all-day picnic and take along the laundry? Nausicaa's half-expressed desire for feminine fulfillment is handled with the same delicacy in Athena's dream visit that the poet displays in his later depiction of the princess's exciting encounter with the flattering Odysseus.

Finally, divine motivation occurs especially at points when a character arrives at a radical change of purpose. I suppose the best example is Achilles' decision to allow Hector's body to be returned to Priam. As so often, the divine command is, strictly speaking, superfluous. If we were to delete all reference to the fact that Thetis has been ordered by Zeus to speak to Achilles, the story would proceed entirely naturally, in line with both social custom and psychological probability. Achilles has done all that he can for Patroclus, both to avenge him and to honor him. The time for mourning is past, but Achilles does not know how, or cannot bring himself, to accept finally the fact of Patroclus's death and life without him. Essentially this is what his mother tells Achilles. She says that he is going too far in his continued defilement of Hector's corpse. It is time to give the body to the Trojans and bring the whole episode to a close.

Although Achilles tells himself that he will receive Priam only in obedience to Thetis's urging and to Zeus's command, Homer makes it plain that his mood and purpose are wholly changed internally. The final scene in which Achilles and the mourning father come to understand, to sympathize with one another, and to weep together over all of human sorrow is abundant proof that Homer wished and knew how to portray an inner transformation in his hero, not simply to accomplish a change by divine fiat.

There has been considerable scholarly debate as to how far Homeric man actually believed that his mental and emotional reactions come to him from an external source. Bruno Snell went so far as to declare that there is in Homer "no genuine reflexion, no dialogue of the soul with itself." Homeric man "does not yet regard himself as the source of his own decisions."[14] This extreme view has been challenged by a number of scholars, most effectively by Albin Lesky.[15] Lesky points out that Homer sometimes provides a double motivation. For example, Diomedes says of Achilles, "He will fight again, whenever the time comes / that the heart in his body urges him to and the god drives him."[16] Often the same character will say at one point that a god was responsible and on another occasion will accept full responsibility himself for what he has done. Or, something which happens especially in Odysseus's narrative, he will say that someone acted either because a god told him to do so or in obedience to his own mind or heart. It is true that the words Homer used to indicate heart, mind, and intelligence were not yet sharply refined in their meaning. Both *phren* and *thymos* can refer to what today we would call emotions or mind or will, but Homer does not distinguish among the three. *Noos* is usually more specifically allied to rationality but is hardly precise. All the same, I believe that Lesky is right in arguing that Homer furnishes us with

14. Bruno Snell, The Discovery of the Mind, trans. T. G. Rosenmeyer (Cambridge, Mass.: Harvard University Press, 1953), pp. 19 and 31.
15. Albin Lesky, Göttliche und menschliche Motivation im homerischen Epos, Sitzungsberichte den Heidelberger Akademie der Wiesenschaften, 4 Abhandlung (June 1961).
16. Homer Iliad 9. 702–3.

ample evidence of self-understanding in his characters. He chooses as a particularly clear instance Achilles' response to the embassy which approached him with both ethical and expediential arguments to persuade him to return to the fighting. Achilles says, "You have said all these things after my own mind [κατὰ θυμόν], but my heart [κραδίη] swells up in anger whenever I remember how the son of Atreus dishonored me before the Argives" (9. 645–48). We may note, too, that sometimes the choice of whether to assume responsibility oneself or to blame something on the gods will be greatly influenced by the particular circumstances in which a character is involved. It is most interesting to compare three occasions when Agamemnon refers to his quarrel with Achilles. Speaking to the assembled leaders, Agamemnon says that Zeus drove him into quarreling. When he is desperate and willing to do anything to bring Achilles back, he exclaims, "I was mad, I will not deny it. . . . I was mad and persuaded by wretched thoughts [ἀασάμην φρεσὶ λευγαλέῃσι πιθήσας]" (9. 116–19). In the final formal reconciliation scene, when he knows that Achilles is fully prepared to lay by the dispute, Agamemnon says that he is not responsible but rather Zeus, Moira, the Erinys, and Ate! (19. 86–87). And later in the same scene, "I was mad, and Zeus took away my senses" (19. 137).

Here there is certainly evidence of "that dialogue of the soul with itself" which Snell denied for Homer. Other passages seem to me to support not only the poet's intuitive psychological acumen, but a specific interest in the nature of thought and emotions. Some of the similes are illustrative here. In contrast to the normal practice of comparing a human attitude or action to something in nature, Homer will, though very rarely, compare an outward external act to something mental. In book 15 in the *Iliad* he says of Hera's rapid flight upward to Olympus that it was "like the darting thought of a man who travels over wide territory as he thinks in his shrewd mind, 'If only I were here or there,' imagining many things."[17] To a degree beyond that of most contemporary novelists and psychologists, Homer

17. Homer uses both *noos* and *phren* in this passage, both referring to the activity of the mind (15. 80–81).

represents his characters as feeling personally responsible for what they do with their emotions. Achilles speaks of holding on to his anger or checking it almost as a person might talk of investing or not investing a sum of money. Nor is he ignorant of how a person can be self-imprisoned by his emotions to the point of morbidity. He describes anger "which makes even the man of great sense grow wrathful, anger which becomes sweeter to him than dripping honey and fills his breast like rising smoke" (18. 108–10). We may recall, too, how Achilles' self-understanding is demonstrated when he gives orders to the maids to wash Hector's body. He makes sure that Priam does not see the fouled corpse lest his anger might lead Achilles to lose control of himself and kill the old man.

Despite all this evidence of introspection, I suspect that Homer and his audience believed that there were some occasions when a person really was possessed or driven by a power beyond himself, a phenomenon not totally alien to human experience even today. Divine motivation helped to explain a man's bewilderment before aspects of himself which he simply could not comprehend otherwise—as when one says, "Whatever could have made me do that? I wasn't myself." Occasionally the god stands for the sudden inspiration so brilliant one feels it must have come from outside oneself; more often it explains—or explains away—what seems utterly contrary to common sense or foreign to one's moral nature. In cases of this kind, where there is no sign of specific intervention from on high, the Homeric character will frequently say, "A god stole his senses from him." The sentence is almost a metaphor.

A most interesting aspect of the scholarly discussion of psychological motivation is the fact that critics have ignored the problem of how the gods themselves are motivated. The truth is that they are motivated exactly like humans. This would be impossible if, like Snell, we held that Homer did not believe the *thymos* and *phren* to be capable of initiating decision. Certainly the poet did not envision a hierarchy in which each god has a higher god standing over him with the Fates at the top whispering guiding counsel in the ear of Zeus. Actually the parallel with mortals is quite precise. Most of the time the gods simply react either spontaneously to the words and actions of others, or they manifest the ideas and feelings which arise from their thymos or phren. For example, we read, "Zeus considered in his phren, . . . and the following plan seemed best to his thymos."[18] On one occasion Athena reproaches Ares in terms remarkably like those used by mortals.

> Madman, crazed of your wits (φρένας), this is ruin! Your ears
> can listen
> still to reality, but your mind (νόος) is gone and your discipline.
>
> [Iliad, 15. 128–29]

She does not, to be sure, ask, "Has a god stolen your senses from you?" But it is implied that Ares is certainly beside himself. Frequently the gods speak of cherishing or letting go their anger, displaying the same kind of inner conflict and self-understanding of emotional states that we observed in Achilles. The fact that even the gods may sometimes change their minds is offered as a reason why humans also should listen to the prayers of suppliants who have angered them. But there is no suggestion that any intermediary is needed other than the suppliant prayers themselves. These perform their function for gods and mortals alike. In one passage the prayers are personified as the daughters of Zeus. If a man will listen to them and show them reverence, they will bless him. If he denies them, they go in supplication to Zeus, asking that he will punish the hardhearted.[19]

Yet the external motivation is not unknown among the gods. It comes, just as with mortals, in a situation so critical that the poet feels that some special explanation is called for. Two examples are particularly interesting. The first is Calypso's resolve to send Odysseus on his way. Hermes tells Calypso that Zeus says she must let Odysseus go. Later she informs Odysseus, without explanation, that he may leave if he likes. Odysseus, in telling his story to the Phaeacians, says, "Either some god told her to let me go, or she had a change of heart." I suspect that the poet perceived that when a radical change of resolution occurs, there is usually some external event to precipitate it, though not necessarily a supernatural one. In this instance our knowledge that Odysseus spends his

18. Homer Iliad 2. 3–5.
19. Homer Iliad 9. 502–12.

days weeping from homesickness and shares the goddess's bed with obvious reluctance would make Calypso's sad dismissal appear inevitable, even without divine intervention.

A second example is the antichastity belt which Hera borrows from Aphrodite in order to seduce Zeus. Homer tells us that the belt contained "love and desire and seductive endearment which steals away the intelligence of even the sensible."[20] Here the power of sex has been projected on to something external. It parallels almost precisely the use of magic in the encounter between Odysseus and Circe where his virility is represented in the moly plant given to him by Hermes and Circe's feminine sexuality in the drugged potion.

The parallel between divine and human passion is brought out specifically in the long passage where Agamemnon excuses himself to Achilles. Agamemnon tells the story of how one day Zeus, after being deluded by Hera into a rash act, threw Ate out of Heaven and told her never to return to Olympus. Since then she has made her dwelling among men and women. Possibly we might interpret this tale as suggesting that Homer believed the gods to be less susceptible to clouded judgment and the devastating effects of passion than mortals. This fond hope is hardly borne out elsewhere in the epics. The gods are so completely human in their complex personalities that they become for us almost as three dimensional as the human actors. It was not because Homer did not understand the human psyche that he used the gods to motivate men and women. Rather he applied his knowledge of psychology in his fascinating portrayal of the Olympians.

On Being a God

We have been considering Homer's gods in terms of their contribution to the literary quality of the epics or their intervention in mortal affairs. There is another concern of the poet's which is quite different. From time to time he seems to raise the question, "What would it be like to be a god?" Often he appears to be simply enjoying the play of imagination for its own sake, inventing details as to what life would be like if one possessed

20. Homer *Iliad* 14. 215–17.

divine powers. He obviously enjoys the thought of descending
through the air in golden chariots with indefatigable immortal
steeds, horses which graze on grass ambrosia expecially furnished by the river Simois. Or if one were a god, one could
have fun flying about in the form of a bird. The ornithological
epiphanies may indeed be partially explained as derived from
the winged daimones of the Mycenaean period. But I suspect
Homer has his gods put on bird shapes partly because of the
demands of realism and the habit of anthropomorphic thinking. Even a god has to get through the air *somehow!* We recall
the "winged words" of Homer. And we may remember that in
the New Testament the Holy Ghost descends in the form of a
dove. The poet's imaginings show many inconsistencies. Nilsson explained these as due, at least in part, to the clash between
religious needs and the growing rationality of man in the age of
Homer. More frequently I think they are due to the discrepancy
between strict religious belief and literary needs. Nilsson
points out that the gods are never quite omniscient, omnipres-
ent, or omnipotent.[21] They cannot be so if they are to interact
with one another anthropomorphically.

Several passages show the poet reflecting more significantly on the quality of divine existence. There is only one scene
in which the deities actually engage in physical conflict with
one another, and it proves to be a ludicrous affair. Supposedly
we are about to witness a major conflict. All that happens,
beyond insulting and boastful words, is that Athena knocks out
Ares and topples the delicate Aphrodite while Hera boxes
Artemis's ears with her own bow. Possibly the scene was added
with the deliberate intent of providing comic relief although
this is rather a modern notion than a Greek one. I am inclined to
suspect that it echoes on the poet's part a feeling of mortal
superiority. The gods are ridiculous because nothing they do to
one another can be very important. Since nothing is irrevoca-
ble, they have nothing to lose.

On a few occasions the poet seems to sympathize with the
gods for all the trouble which human beings cause them
though the sympathy may be mingled with a touch of pride.
One such passage comes close to being ironic. Dione comforts

21. Nilsson, *History of Greek Religion*, pp. 148 ff.

her daughter Aphrodite, who has just been wounded by
Diomedes, by reciting a long list of all the dreadful things
which gods have been forced to endure because of mortals.
Dione goes on to say that men who fight against the gods ultimately come to a bad end and says that Diomedes will too. As a
matter of fact, Diomedes, at least in the best established version
of his history, was one of the few Homeric heroes to die peacefully at a ripe old age.

Scenes of real poignancy occur when gods allow themselves to care deeply for particular mortals. There is true pathos
in Zeus's pity for Achilles' immortal horses weeping for the
dead Patroclus.

> Poor wretches,
> why then did we ever give you to the lord Peleus,
> a mortal man, and you yourselves are immortal and ageless?
> Only so that among unhappy men you also might be grieved?
> Since among all creatures that breathe on earth and crawl on it
> there is not anywhere a thing more dismal than man is.
>
> [Iliad, 17. 442–47]

Zeus's lament over the death of his son Sarpedon is tragic. He
has suffered an absolute loss. Nothing can console the god,
who experiences at this moment a truly mortal grief. The poet
bestows his human pity on the gods. In the Christian passion
God does not mourn for his son, for this death is but the pre-
lude to resurrection. On the other hand, we have in this event a
possible parallel to the Greek notion that gods must withdraw
at the moment of a mortal's death—in the words, "My God,
why hast thou forsaken me?"

One of the most interesting of all these attempts to see the
relations between gods and mortals from the immortal point of
view, is found in the consolation which Athena offers to Ares
when he has lost his son Ascalaphus. By now, she says, some
other man better than he has died or is about to die. It is a hard
and painful thing to be rescuing all the generations of men. The
gods cannot emotionally afford to be too much concerned
about mortals because, pitiful as they are, there are just too
many of them; there's no end to it! This notion is curiously
paralleled in a contemporary attempt to imagine anthropomorphically the reaction of a divine being. In the rock opera *Jesus*

Christ Superstar, Jesus is surrounded by a crowd of sick and afflicted who beg to be cured. Jesus complains that there are too many of them and too little of him. Almost petulantly he orders the people not to push and crowd him, but to heal themselves.[22]

I have avoided the problem of Fate in this discussion. It is too large a subject to touch peripherally, and it is not strictly germane to my theme. Yet since I have raised the question of whether the Homeric individual believed himself to act on his own responsibility or to be manipulated by external forces, I may state (without discussion) that I am in agreement here with the position of most recent scholars. That is, I completely reject the view that gods and mortals alike are controlled by some higher destiny. Conclusive evidence against a fatalistic determinism may be found in the words of Zeus himself, who, on at least three occasions, quite obviously regards it as possible for him to go against what is "fated" and refrains only because he foresees the dire consequences which would ensue if he broke his agreement with the other gods.[23] Even by the most extreme interpretation, Fate in the epics seems to be the equivalent of the Calvinist foreknowledge which is not the same as predeterminism. Certainly the gods are free, and I have tried to show that in spite of their predilection for meddling, they do not make mortals into puppets. Men and women are basically responsible for their destinies except as they come into conflict with one another and insofar as we are all dependent on chance events in a world which we cannot control. Homeric man tended to explain inexplicable happenings by invoking divine intervention, but this does not seem to have made him feel that he was thereby rendered powerless. One of the touching things in the *Iliad* is the number of occasions when a hero declares, "Well, since the gods appear to be no longer on our side, we must fight all the harder."

It has seemed strange to me that students who feel that the gods make Homer's heroes into nothing but puppets can with equanimity accept determinism in their psychology classes

22. Andrew Lloyd Webber and Tim Rice, *Jesus Christ Superstar. A Rock Opera* (Decca Records, 1970). I am unable to quote the lines verbatim because permission to do so could not be obtained from MCA Music.
23. Cf. Grube, "Divine World of the Odyssey."

without any sense that their human dignity has been impaired. I should like to suggest that they read the following passage from B. F. Skinner, mentally substituting "divine intervention" for "causes."

> The hypothesis that man is not free is essential to the application of scientific method to the study of human behavior. The free inner man who is held responsible for his behavior is only a pre-scientific substitute for the kinds of causes which are discovered in the course of scientific analysis. All these alternative causes lie *outside* the individual.[24]

I hope that I have shown that this sort of description simply will not do for Homeric man.

If, when all is said and done, we feel that there remains some slight discrepancy between the poet's understanding of human behavior and his religious belief, this is the same inconsistency which we find displayed by generations of Christian believers. The Christian says, "It was God's will that he died of the plague." Homer says, "Athena killed him—by the spear of Achilles."

24. Carl R. Rogers quotes this passage as an example of the strict determinism of behavioristic psychology. Skinner made the statement in 1953. Rogers does not name the work in which it first appeared. See his *Freedom to Learn* (Columbus: Charles E. Merrill Publishing Co., 1969), p. 260.

The Case of Sosia *versus* Sosia

The history of Greek religion testifies to innumerable instances in which one of the Olympian gods or goddesses replaced or absorbed a local deity. We see traces of the religious evolution in the epithets or second names of the god (for example, Phoebus Apollo or Zeus Meilichios), in the peculiar rites which are associated with a deity's worship in particular places, and in various myths which have converted the historical process into fascinating narratives of individual rivalries and erotic unions. One of the most frequent types is the tale of Zeus's amours with mortal women. Even his marriage with Hera perhaps reflects a concession to the demands of the worshipers of the great earth goddess of Argos, who was established long before Zeus was ever heard of in Greece. This may have been accompanied by the divorce, so to speak, of his first wife, Dione, henceforth relegated to the role of Zeus's mistress and mother of Aphrodite.[1] Echoes of earlier gods whom Zeus replaced as the lover, or sometimes as the father, of a local figure are numerous. Helen, for example, was often referred to as the daughter of Tyndareus although everyone knew the story of her birth from the egg which Leda laid after her encounter with Zeus in the form of a swan.

The most interesting of such accounts concerns the birth of Heracles. Even his mother, Alcmena, believed that his father

1. Guthrie discusses this and other theories of the origin and ultimate union of Zeus and Hera (*The Greeks and Their Gods*, pp. 66 ff.). The replacement of Dione (or Dia) by Hera was first suggested by A. B. Cook.

was Amphitryon when all the time it was Zeus. Of all the tricks and disguises which Zeus employed to carry on his philanderings, the device of appearing to a woman in the form of her own husband was perhaps the most tasteless and the most imaginative—as well as the most likely to succeed. For us the first dramatic presentation of this divine impersonation is Plautus's *Amphitryon*, produced at Rome in the early part of the second century B.C. How much Plautus modified or added to his Greek source we cannot possibly know. As it stands, *Amphitryon* is a strange mixture of mythological burlesque and satiric realism.

The play opens at the point when Amphitryon is about to return from his war with the Teleboans. Jupiter has come to Alcmena with news of the victory and presents to her a golden cup which he (i.e., Amphitryon) had won by his heroic exploits. He is accompanied by Mercury, who has assumed the form of Amphitryon's slave, Sosia. Shortly afterwards the real Amphitryon is not only confronted with the news that someone has made him a cuckold but is reproached by his wife for what seems to her unjustified charges and insane behavior on his part. He is mocked by the disguised Mercury and otherwise tormented, both physically and psychologically, until—with a rapid shift of dramatic mood—awesome signs come from Heaven and Amphitryon learns that Jupiter has proclaimed himself cofather with Amphitryon of newly born twins.

In his prologue to *Amphitryon* Plautus tells us that this play is a tragicomedy. For it would not be right, he says, for gods and kings to appear in a play which was nothing but comedy; yet neither can it be wholly tragedy since important parts are given to slaves (59–63). Without worrying particularly about Plautus's social attitudes as reflected here, critics have generally agreed with his literary judgment. The *Amphitryon*, although not as obviously a problem play as Menander's *The Arbitration*, for example, or Terence's *The Brothers*, has a more serious undercurrent than most of Plautus's work. For both proof and explanation, critics have been fond of pointing to Alcmena, whose situation and character are portrayed with almost tender understanding and sympathy.[2]

2. For examples of this critical view cf. the following:
"There is unalloyed fun in Sosia's bewilderment on finding another Sosia as like him 'as milk is like milk.' One does not know whether to marvel more at

I should like to propose two further theses. First, I believe that the real reason for the ambivalent nature of the *Amphitryon* is that the underlying theme of the play is such that the deeper meaning cannot be entirely disregarded, no matter how much it may be subjected to comic treatment. This theme is, of course, the problem of self-identity. Second, I maintain that the truly tragicomic figure is the slave Sosia.

Certain serious questions suggest themselves (whether or not Plautus specifically formulated them to himself) even without Sosia. If, for example, Alcmena was perfectly content with the appearance and outward manners of Jupiter, then was it really Amphitryon whom she loved, or not? Or as Alcmena despairingly asks, is there any point in knowing the truth if one cannot communicate it to anyone? If Plautus had chosen to develop all the implications of his plot in the persons of Alcmena and Amphitryon, he would have risked finding himself with a pure tragedy on his hands. As it is, the difficulties of the hero and heroine are in a sense externalized. Even Amphitryon, at least in the mutilated form of the play which has come down to us, never has any self-doubts. He resents the imposter; he suspects that witchcraft may have been used against Alcmena. But he knows always that he is the true Amphitryon and that Jupiter is not. It is Sosia who really confronts the psychological dilemma, who knows that he is himself and yet faces evidence proving that he is not. It is Sosia, in short, who bumps up against himself, who sees himself coming, who discovers that he is his own worst enemy!

It is important to remember that when the disguised Mercury is about to accost Sosia, he assumes not only Sosia's appearance but his character. This means that even within the

---

Roman toleration for such representation of the gods, or at the author's introduction in such surroundings of his sweetest and purest woman. Alcmena's character is apparent in her unaffected grief over parting from her husband, her love of virtue, and conscious freedom from wilful guilt. Her spotless honesty makes the supreme god a charlatan" (J. Wight Duff, *A Literary History of Rome from the Origins to the Close of the Golden Age* [New York: Barnes and Noble, 1960], p. 129).

"The arrival of Sosia to announce his master's return leads to an amusing low comedy scene in which the slave is almost convinced by Mercury that he has lost his identity. . . . [Alcmena] is a devoted wife and a person of honor and dignity; she is the noblest woman character in Plautine comedy" (George E. Duckworth, *The Nature of Roman Comedy: A Study in Popular Entertainment* [Princeton: Princeton University Press, 1952], p. 150).

comic framework it is actually a confrontation of Sosia by Sosia. What Plautus is doing is presenting to us literally the picture of the human personality which we (and Plautus too) have long been accustomed to accept in metaphor. Thus we see that Sosia is in conflict with himself; he has difficulty in understanding himself; he tries—but in vain—to lie to himself. In words of the twentieth century we may say that his is the problem of every man; that is, ultimately he is a stranger to himself. Now the trick of taking literally that which is meant metaphorically is one of Plautus's favorite comic techniques, and I have no doubt that the laughter of the audience is his goal in the Sosia scenes as everywhere else. Yet the interesting fact remains that Sosia's progressive bewilderment and his continually frustrated attempts to get out of his dilemma parallel step by step the argumentation of philosophers concerned with the problem of self-identity.

Like any good philosopher Plautus follows a logical development. Sosia's first problem is the realization of himself in the third person. Mercury has just said that he hears somebody (*nescio quis*) talking. And Sosia exclaims, "I'm saved! He doesn't see me. He says *Somebody* is talking, but *my* name is certainly Sosia" (331–32). The first perception that one is or has a self, and a self that is limited, must logically occur at that moment when one recognizes that one is external and an object to another self. Ordinarily there is something in us which resists this object-status, but here Sosia comically takes refuge in the idea that the neutral designation "somebody" cannot possibly apply to his own highly personal self. He is not just "somebody"; he is Sosia. Of course still worse is in store for him. He is not merely an object to the personal reflections of another "somebody"; he is an object to Sosia.

Sosia never loses the inner conviction that he is still the same person he had always thought himself to be; and he comes very close to asserting the Cartesian "*Cogito, ergo sum.*" "But when I think, then I am certainly the same as I have always been" (447). What he lacks is any rational proof, and he recognizes rightly that Descartes's conclusion is conviction and *not* proof. The tests he applies are those which any philosopher, or even any human being, would naturally think of.

First of all, Sosia associates his sense of identity with his physical body. Mercury has just called him mad, and Sosia tries to prove his sanity to himself by carefully recalling recent events, concluding with his vivid awareness of the sensations of the moment.

> Am I not right now standing in front of our house? Isn't this a lantern in my hand? Didn't this man just now beat me up? By heaven, he did! For my jaw still hurts from it! So what am I worrying about? Why don't I go straight inside?
>
> [445–48]

In a sense this approach produces Sosia's strongest evidence: present sensations, especially those stemming from remembered events. His awareness of himself as tied to a body which has never ceased to provide a continuing stream of sensation, a body whose presence is felt as a part of every reaction, no matter what—this is the one thing which nobody can take away from him. Consequently he never ceases to feel that he is and has been one Sosia. Unfortunately, however, a feeling is untransferable, and Sosia's inability to prove the reality of what he so strongly feels adds to his sense of frustration.

Sosia's second test is the appeal to objects in the outside world. He demands that Mercury describe for him the Teleboans' gift to Amphitryon and the appearance of Amphitryon's seal. Here, of course, Sosia fails since Mercury's description is accurate even in the smallest details. There is still more spectacular failure when the cup in question is found to be already in Alcmena's possession although the seal on its former container is intact. This attempt on Sosia's part is less convincing for him than the inner assurance of his own sensations. But it has the advantage of offering a common point of reference for himself and for his audience. Sosia searches for confirmation in his surroundings just as one who has fainted seeks to orient himself by means of the familiar "Where am I?" He appeals to things as guarantees in the way that we all do dozens of times a day. For example, "Of course I locked the door. See, it's bolted." Or, "Yes, I've finished my paper. Read it!" Unfortunately Plautus tricks poor Sosia by bringing in the supernatural. Otherwise his scientific reliance on matter to behave consistently would have worked. But there is always some slight element of uncertainty in an appeal to objects. One's memory may have failed. Or someone may have intervened secretly. Or nature itself may not be quite as we have pronounced it to be.

For a third try Sosia takes refuge in the belief that only he can know what he has done in secret. But, as it turns out, this other Sosia knows that during the battle Sosia hid in his tent and drank a whole jug of wine straight! Such an assertion might well drive anyone mad and should excuse completely the apparently incoherent babbling with which Sosia so irritates Amphitryon later in the play. If Mercury were conceived as another mortal, then of course the situation would be impossible. Without the gods, one would never be forced to face the problem of identity in quite this way. If, however, we look at the conflict as being carried on between two aspects of Sosia's own self, then we see that Plautus is giving us a sharply drawn picture of a man's attempt and failure to hide from himself the memory of his ignoble behavior at a time of crisis.

Sosia's final summing up of the situation is again significant in terms of a man's struggle within himself rather than as an effort to prove his identity to someone else. By now he realizes that the stranger is "as much like me as I am" (tam consimilest atque ego). He looks and acts like Sosia, has all of Sosia's knowledge and memories. The reaction of the original Sosia at this point is a curious one. All three of his tests having failed to some extent at least, he is forced by his own reasoning to admit that the man before the house is Sosia. But his inward emotional conviction is so strong that he never admits (save for an instant at the very moment of being beaten) that he himself is not Sosia. As a result he holds on to both ideas and almost drives his master mad by referring to both Sosias in the first person singular and yet speaking of them as being two separate people.

So far we have been concerned only with Sosia's efforts to find a way out of his difficulty. I should like now to point out several broader implications of the story, stemming partly from the myth itself and partly from Plautus's peculiar treatment of it. At this point it does not really matter whether or not Plautus was consciously aware of these interpretations, for the point which I am trying to make is that there is in the tale so true an insight into the human condition that even if Plautus had been incapable of seeing more than the comic possibilities, the play would have evoked somber overtones.

In the broadest sense, of course, Amphitryon poses the unanswerable question: just what is it which makes the Self? If another has my appearance, my personality, my memories, is there anything which prevents me from concluding that he is Me? And if I can reply to this question only by pointing to my own lively sense that I and I alone am Me, then what if the Other should reply in similar fashion? Granted that the dilemma is couched in impossible terms, the fact is that if I cannot resolve it, I am forced to acknowledge that the self, my own self, remains a mystery.

Another and quite different aspect of human experience is suggested by Sosia's meeting up with his double upon his return home after a prolonged expedition abroad. For anyone who has made an abrupt break in the course of his life, who has gone away and changed as the result of new experiences, who has developed hitherto unsuspected facets of his character—for any such person Sosia's position should be familiar. Let us forget Mercury for a moment and look at what Sosia would have experienced without him. For the slave returning from the great adventure there would certainly be a brief moment when he would not quite be ready to step into the old role, when he might well insist, "I'm not that same old Sosia you used to know." For any person picking up an old way of life after distance in time or space, it is easy to feel that there is a familiar self waiting to claim one, a self which has been there all the time and which is presently so real as to seem to deny the reality of anything experienced away from it. This sense that an established system of patterned reactions and habits exists almost as a separate self which one must decide whether or not to recognize may appear either as threat or temptation, but I believe that the experience is universal. In Plautus's play this interpretation is suggested by Mercury's answer when Sosia asks who he is if he is not Sosia. "When I don't want to be Sosia, why then you be Sosia if you like. But now when I am Sosia, you'll be beaten, you scum, if you don't make off!" (439–40).

I have spoken already of the meeting of the two Sosias as representing a struggle within the self. The conflict also assumes the form of a self-judgment with Mercury on the bench. I have mentioned Sosia's unsuccessful attempts at lying. I refer, of course, to Sosia's intention of giving what purported to be an eyewitness account of a battle and Mercury's forestalling him by reminding him that he was actually hiding and can speak only from hearsay. In a broader sense he not only pronounces himself guilty but assigns and administers his own punishment. There is a significant passage just before Sosia first perceives Mercury:

Sosia. I'm one slave who should get a beating. I wasn't too anxious, was I, to think about paying my respects to the gods and thanking them as I should for my safe arrival? By God, if they paid me back my deserts, they would commission some man to bash my face in properly since they've got no thanks for all the good they did me.
Mercury. This fellow does what not many people do. He recognizes what he deserves.

[180–85]

These lines are important as indicating that Sosia is not an innocent victim of the brutal stranger. He receives precisely the sentence which he has just passed on himself. Moreover, the one who administers the punishment is doubly Sosia's own self: first, Mercury is physically Sosia's counterpart and claims his very name; second, Mercury decides upon his conduct by asking himself what Sosia would do if their roles were reversed.

Since I have taken on his shape and appearance, I should make my deeds and character like his too. So I must be a sly and clever rascal and drive him away from the house with his own weapons—rouguery

[265–69]

It is a well-established psychological principle that inwardly one adopts the same basic attitude toward oneself (hostility, anxiety, acceptance) that one is accustomed to direct toward the outside world and other people. Thus it is not inappropriate that Mercury as Sosia should deal with the returning Sosia as the latter would have behaved given the strength and opportunity.

Finally, there is just one more aspect of human experience which I believe lies back of the story of Sosia's encounter with himself. This is that uneasy sense that in some way the Self comprises more than the conscious ego. What this "something more" is, nobody has ever proved, at least not to the satisfaction of everyone else, but I am convinced that the Greeks and Romans were in varying degrees aware of it. There are hints in Plato and the dramatists. Plotinus surely had it in mind in the All-Soul. I believe that it is back of the concepts of the Greek Daimon and the Roman Genius.

If we try to explain why the people of antiquity developed the idea of a sort of guardian *alter ego* or greater self, which lived out one's life with one, our explanation will depend upon our philosophical and psychological affiliations. If we prefer to keep the Greeks and Romans free of any contamination with later theories, we may say that the individual's constant awareness of the society around him led him to introject the social milieu, as it were, and posit a second self as the ever-present observer. For the Freudians, of course, there are the unconscious id and super-ego. In this connection E. R. Dodds has utilized the theory of the unconscious to explain metempsychosis, which he believes to be derived from our dim sense of there being somewhere within us forgotten and repressed materials which influence us without our being aware of when or how.[3] In the same way it is possible that the Genius and the Daimon reflect a man's vague knowledge of the unconscious part of himself. The Jungian school of psychology might give a similar explanation but with the difference that the unconscious would be not personal but racial, the collective unconscious of all mankind. Novelists also have suggestions to offer. D. H. Lawrence, for example, presents the idea that there is a basic blood consciousness, far deeper and more extensive than the mental ego, and that here only can a man really find himself. Finally (though the list is not exhaustive) Jean-Paul Sartre

3. E. R. Dodds, *The Greeks and the Irrational* (Berkeley: University of California Press, 1951), pp. 151–52. More specifically, Dodds says that the idea of rebirth sprang from "the need to rationalize those unexplained feelings of guilt which . . . were prevalent in the Archaic Age. Men were, I suppose, dimly conscious—and on Freud's view, rightly conscious—that such feelings had their roots in a submerged and long-forgotten past experience."

has rejected entirely the concept of the unconscious but insists that the ego of man is secondary to a nonpersonalized consciousness and that here we find the wellspring of a human freedom so absolute that nothing in the way of heredity or environment can predict its course.[4]

But the problem of what we ourselves are to give as the explanation of the Self is far removed from the study of *Amphitryon*. Furthermore, Plautus, even among writers of comedy, is one of the least philosophically minded. As I said earlier, I am not trying to prove that he was conscious of all these implications as I have discussed them. Possibly he was simply adapting a Greek source and copied without full understanding. Or perhaps his observation of human behavior has been so accurate that his characters seem real to us and hence challenge us to look for more than Plautus himself realized. Any great comedian must be in some sense a psychologist in order to perceive the foibles and the ridiculous traits of our fellow human beings and in order to make us see them. In the character of Sosia and the adventure which befalls him, Plautus has exploited the humorous possibilities to the fullest. He examines in the form of a literal projection almost every conceivable way in which a person can try to take an objective point of view on himself. Plautus, I believe—but if not he, then his Greek predecessor—has grasped intuitively the realization that Sosia's dilemma is in essence that of every man—in short, the human condition.

We must conclude then that in the case of Sosia *versus* Sosia it appears impossible to arrive at any satisfactory decision. In the first place how can one possibly determine which Sosia is the defendant? Moreover it seems clear that the guilty party is really the gods, who started the trouble by allotting but one form to two persons. Unfortunately the gods do not usually acknowledge the jurisdiction of the human court.

4. It is not appropriate in this discussion to attempt a full treatment of Greek and Roman concepts of the Self. The most obvious examples would be Euripides' internalization of the Erinyes' pursuit of Orestes, and even better, Plato's analysis of the tripartite soul in books 4 and 9 of the *Republic*. Terence's play, *The Self-Tormentor* (*Heautontimoroumenos*) certainly suggests that the Greek New Comedy was interested in the problem of a man's relation to himself.

Index of Authors and Titles

139